COOKING
THE SCANDINAVIAN WAY

Uniform with this volume

COOKING THE ITALIAN WAY
Dorothy Daly

COOKING THE GERMAN WAY
Nella Whitfield

COOKING THE AUSTRIAN WAY
Ann Knox

COOKING THE CHINESE WAY
Nina Froud

COOKING THE SPANISH WAY
Elsa Behrens

COOKING THE CZECH WAY
Joža Břízová

COOKING THE RUSSIAN WAY
Musia Soper

COOKING THE FRENCH WAY
Elizabeth Smart and Agnes Ryan

COOKING THE JEWISH WAY
Ann Wald

COOKING THE
SCANDINAVIAN
WAY

ELNA ADLERBERT

SPRING BOOKS · LONDON

Contents

Introduction

There was a time when Scandinavian food habits were largely conditioned by the climate, which limited the supply of fresh food to a few months of the year. As a result, meals tended to be rather monotonous, and salted fish or meat with potatoes was served most of the time. But things are very different today, and Scandinavian specialities like smorgasbord and Swedish meatballs are popular all over the world. If you are the kind of cook who enjoys trying something rather different you will, I hope, find many new ideas in this book.

Scandinavian cooking as we know it today really began to develop in the eighteenth century. At that time France exerted a great influence on Scandinavia, and its culture even penetrated to the kitchens. At first, this influence was felt only in the upper strata of society, which could afford to experiment with more exotic foods and sometimes even went so far as to import French cooks. But in time, better communications and methods of food preservation made it possible for the general public to take advantage of this widened scope, and the French influence is still present in Scandinavian cuisine.

The Scandinavians are a rather taciturn and formal people, and have preserved a ritualistic tradition round their eating habits in spite of being progressive in many other spheres. Thus almost every festivity has its own traditional menu, which will be faithfully adhered to in every home. On each Tuesday during Lent there is a standard dessert of buns with almond cream and milk. Easter Eve is celebrated with smorgasbord and boiled eggs, at which time there is usually a competition in the family to see which child can eat the most eggs. I remember stuffing myself with eggs until I was nearly sick, trying to compete with my older brother, who had an apparently unlimited capacity, and was always the winner in the end.

In the middle of August the crayfish season starts. As crayfish have become quite rare, they are only allowed to be caught for one month of the year. They are a superb delicacy and a good reason in most families for at least one party during this open season. These parties are nearly always held out of doors. The evenings are then fairly dark, in contrast with midsummer, when it stays light all through the night. It is therefore customary to hang coloured lanterns around the table, which light it up and enhance the sight of the startlingly red crayfish, before the more serious business of eating and drinking begins.

The Name Day for Martin Luther is the 11th November. This day is celebrated by southern Swedes and Danes with a roast goose dinner. Scandinavians are very careful never to waste any food, and consequently the whole of the animal must be used. In the case of a goose, the blood is drawn and made into a soup. This soup has a unique flavour, which, I am afraid, can only be appreciated by those who are accustomed to it from childhood; but for the Danes, it is a delicacy not to be missed on this festive occasion. The recipe has not been included in this book for practical reasons, as the goose has to be slaughtered in a special way in order to collect the blood for this soup.

Christmas is the main festival of the year, and it has a special significance for Scandinavians. In pagan days there was a midwinter festival at this time, which is the darkest period of the year. In the northern parts, there is no daylight at all, and even as far south as Denmark the days are very short indeed. To relieve this dreary period, an atmosphere of light and gaiety is created, a custom which must stem from a deeply rooted need in our nature. The season is ushered in by the Lucia festival, which celebrates the Queen of Light. Although this is Christian in origin, as St. Lucia brought light in a spiritual sense to Scandinavia, there is very little in this festival to remind us of anything associated with the Church. Scandinavians are not particularly religious and, for most of them, these celebrations are more important for traditional reasons than as reminders of religious faith.

The Lucia festival occurs on the 13th December. A female member of each family then dresses in a white gown, wears a crown of lighted candles, and wakes the family in the early morning with the Lucia song, carrying a tray with coffee and Lucia buns. It is celebrated in the same way in schools and various institutions, where the prettiest girl is selected to be Lucia. It has in fact developed into a major beauty contest in Sweden, where each district selects a Lucia, and from them the national Queen of Light is chosen.

It is after this festival that, in most families, the real preparation for Christmas begins. In the old days this meant, first of all, the slaughter of the Christmas pig. In farm districts this is still done, and every part of the pig is utilised. The blood is made into sausages, the feet and head are jellied, the ham is salted and the offal is made into various pâtés and puddings. These dishes are all served during the Christmas season and are not likely to be prepared again for another year. Nowadays most people, of course, buy these delicacies already prepared.

That the pig still has special significance is evident from biscuits and marzipan sweets which are made in its shape only at Christmas time. Baking special cakes is a feature in every family's Christmas preparation. It is entered into with great enthusiasm by most children, who are usually allowed to shape and decorate at least some part of the biscuit dough.

Christmas Eve is most important, as it is then that the presents are given out. In many districts a simple noonday meal consisting of soup and sausages, both made from the slaughtered pig, is served. A special bread is sliced and soaked in the soup. This meal originated as a means of saving time, in order to be better able to prepare for the evening's festivities, when the meal consists of a fish dish followed by rice porridge. The fish is bought dried and has to be marinated several weeks before it is boiled and served with special sauce and mustard. It is also customary to place an unpeeled almond in the porridge. The person who gets this almond in his portion is said to be the one to marry during the following year, a superstition which occurs in many countries in different forms.

After this meal the tree is lighted, Christmas songs are sung and everyone joins hands to dance around the tree. Then the presents are given out by someone dressed up as Santa Claus. In some parts it is believed that little gnomes live about the house. In order to please them and ensure their help for the coming year, many people set plates of porridge in the attic or cellar on Christmas Eve, hoping that the gnomes will partake joyfully of the meal.

On Christmas Day ham is always served, but the garnishing varies. After that, New Year's Day is usually celebrated with parties, at which the Christmas menu is repeated.

Though most countries have their traditional and seasonal meals, the Scandinavians go a bit further. For it is not only in this way that their adherance to table ritual is manifest. An individual meal has its special formalities, mainly to do with drinking. The traditional drink is 'snaps' or aquavit, which is served with the smorgasbord. Only when the host holds up his filled glass may the guests lift theirs. One must not, however, start drinking until one has joined in a song, at the end of which the word 'skol' is spoken in response to the host's 'skol', whereupon the glass is drained in one gulp. The glasses are then half refilled, and the whole ritual is repeated. It is a tremendous *faux pas* to drink in a haphazard manner, and there are strict rules about who may invite whom to a 'skol'. These rules, oddly enough, do not apply to beer, which can also be served with smorgasbord, but they apply to wine, served with the other courses. It is also important to hold the glass in the right position, close to the region of the heart. One must then look straight into the eyes of the person one is drinking with, both before the glass is drained and afterwards, when the glass is again lowered to the same position before being replaced on the table. This ritual is so ingrained that it is performed quite naturally by most Scandinavians.

There are also rules about thanking the hostess for the meal. On formal occasions, this is done by the guest seated on the left side of the hostess, who makes a little speech of appreciation on the part of all present. But on all occasions each guest must go up to the hostess on leaving the table, thanking her for the food.

You will gather from this that the Scandinavian takes the pleasures of eating very seriously. He believes that the gathering together of friends and family for a festive meal is an occasion to be marked by dignity and ceremony. Perhaps the climate and the relative isolation of Scandinavia engenders this attitude. The customs may seem strange to the foreigner, but one must remember that they have developed as an expression of the pleasure to be derived from company. The rituals serve to enhance the festive mood and their enactment forms a bond between the participants.

Special Ingredients

Most of the ingredients required for these recipes are readily available in England and elsewhere. Many of the larger food stores stock Scandinavian tinned goods such as herrings, anchovies, cranberries, mussels, etc. A variety of Scandinavian hard bread of the biscuit type can also be obtained, this being used for serving smorgasbord.

The only thing you might have difficulty in obtaining is fresh dill, which is very seldom used in English cooking, and one way of ensuring a continuous supply is to grow one's own. It is an easy herb to cultivate and will flourish in a window box if a garden is not available. The seeds can be obtained in any shop specialising in herbs and spices.

Equipment

Although no special equipment is necessary, there are a few things which will facilitate cooking the Scandinavian way. I would recommend investing in one large and one small cast iron pot, with tight-fitting lids. These pots are now very attractively designed so that they can be brought straight to the table without spoiling the general décor. They can be placed directly on the flame as well as in the oven, i.e. for browning meat or vegetables and for slow cooking.

I would also recommend the purchase of a Scandinavian birch whisk, obtainable at any large store which stocks Continental furniture. These whisks make quite a difference to the ease with which you can prepare smooth sauces. Once you have tried one, you will certainly not want to do without it.

Apart from these items you will need what all good housewives usually have; wooden spoons, a good steel whisk, chopping bowl, rolling pin, etc.

Useful Facts and Figures

COMPARISON OF ENGLISH AND AMERICAN WEIGHTS AND MEASURES

English weights and measures have been used in most of the recipes in this book. The following table gives their conversions into cups and tablespoons. American cups are standard '½-pint' measuring cups, but the American pint is smaller than the British, and American ½-pint cups are actually equivalent to two-fifths of a British pint.

Liquid Measure

One pint of liquid may be regarded as equal to two American measuring cups for all practical purposes.
3 teaspoons equal 1 tablespoon.
16 tablespoons equal 1 cup.

Solid Measure

ENGLISH	AMERICAN
1 lb. Butter or other fat	2 cups
1 lb. Flour	4 cups
1 lb. Granulated or Castor Sugar	2 cups
1 lb. Brown (moist) Sugar	2⅓ cups
1 lb. Icing or Confectioner's Sugar	3 cups
1 lb. Syrup or Treacle	1 cups
1 lb. Dried Fruit	2 cups
1 lb. Chopped Meat (finely packed)	2 cups
1 lb. Lentils or Split Peas	2 cups
1 lb. Coffee (unground)	2⅔ cups
1 lb. Breadcrumbs	4 cups
½ oz. Flour	1 level tablespoon
1 oz. Flour	1 heaped tablespoon
1 oz. Syrup or Treacle	1 tablespoon
1 oz. Sugar	1 level tablespoon
1 oz. Jam or Jelly	1 level tablespoon
½ oz. Butter	1 tablespoon smoothed off

FRENCH MEASURES

It is difficult to convert to French measurements with absolute accuracy, since 1 oz. is equivalent to 28·352 grammes. The table below is therefore very approximate.

Liquid Measure

Approximately 1¾ pints may be regarded as equal to 1 litre. 1 demilitre is half a litre, and 1 décilitre is one-tenth of a litre.

Solid Measure

1 oz. is equal to approximately 30 grammes.
Approximately 2 lb. 3 oz. is equal to 1 kilogramme.

COOKING TEMPERATURES

Water

    Simmering 180° F.
    Boiling   212° F.

Oven Temperatures	*Electricity* °F.	*Gas Regulo No.*
COOL	225—250	$0-\frac{1}{2}$
VERY SLOW	250—275	$\frac{1}{2}-1$
SLOW	275—300	1—2
VERY MODERATE	300—350	2—3
MODERATE	350—375	4
MODERATELY HOT	375—400	5
HOT	400—450	6—7
VERY HOT	450—500	8—9

Note: This table is an approximate guide only. Different makes of cooker vary and if you are in any doubt about setting it is as well to refer to the manufacturer's temperature chart.

To convert °F. to °C., subtract 32° and multiply by $\frac{5}{9}$.

To convert °C. to °F., multiply by $\frac{9}{5}$ and add 32°.

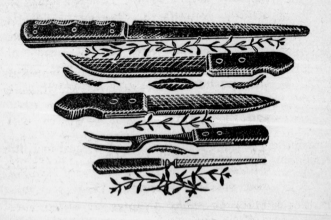

SMORGASBORD DISHES

The smorgasbord plays an important rôle in Scandinavian food culture. It is known all the world over and is often the first thing that comes to people's minds when thinking of Scandinavian cooking. The word actually means sandwich table, and bread and butter are of course always provided, though not necessarily eaten by everyone.

The extent of the smorgasbord depends very much on the occasion: it can vary in quantity from just a few tit-bits to a sumptuous table laden with every variety of cold food available. If you have a small smorgasbord it is served at the table where you will be seated for the entire meal. In that case it usually consists of different kinds of herring served with boiled potatoes, cheese, butter and several kinds of bread. On the other hand the large smorgasbord is set out on a separate table, to which you go to choose what you like before sitting down to eat. Traditionally the smorgasbord is only the introduction to the meal, and is followed at least by a main course and dessert. Nowadays there is a tendency to make simpler arrangements and the main course may be left out.

When entertaining a large number of guests it can be both convenient and festive to serve smorgasbord. Most of the dishes can be prepared beforehand, and some, which are bought ready-made in tins, need only to be arranged and decorated. But it is important that a good smorgasbord be both plentiful and varied, and one must not under-estimate the time and care needed for its preparation. It is usual to have many kinds of herring, cold meats, poultry and fish. Smoked eel, salmon and shellfish are generally included on more festive occasions. A variety of salads is essential, as well as different kinds of cheeses. In Scandinavia it is also customary to provide one or two hot dishes, for example little sausages with fried potatoes or a tasty casserole. It is important to cater for everyone's taste, so I have tried to give as varied a selection of recipes as possible from which to choose.

HERRING IN MUSTARD SAUCE

Swedish

8 SERVINGS

4 salted herring fillets
5 tablespoons vinegar
2 tablespoons water
1½ tablespoons French mustard
2 tablespoons sugar

4 tablespoons oil
4 tablespoons chopped
gherkins
1 hard-boiled egg
1 tablespoon chopped chives

Soak herring fillets in cold water overnight. Dry and remove skins. Place in a bowl and pour over vinegar mixed with water. Let them marinate for 2—6 hours. Remove fillets, cut into inch wide strips and arrange on a shallow serving dish. Put mustard in a bowl and add sugar and oil. Stir together until light and creamy. Then stir in chopped gherkins. Pour this sauce over herrings. Chop egg finely and sprinkle on top together with chopped chives. Serve with small boiled new potatoes.

GLASSBLOWER'S HERRING

Swedish

6 SERVINGS

2 salt herrings
1 tablespoon crushed allspice
2 bayleaves
½ teaspoon mustard seed
1 teaspoon grated horseradish

2 onions, sliced
½ carrot, sliced
4 tablespoons water
½ pint vinegar
3 oz. sugar

Clean fish and remove heads. Wash and put to soak in cold water for about 12 hours. Drain and dry. Slice across, in ½-inch pieces, leaving in bone. Place in glass jar in layers with spices, horseradish, onions and carrot. Put vinegar, water and sugar in saucepan and bring to the boil. Chill and pour into jar. It should cover the herring completely. Cover jar and place in refrigerator for at least 12 hours, but the longer the better. Serve directly from the jar.

PICKLED SALT HERRING

Swedish

4—6 SERVINGS

1 large salt herring
¼ pint vinegar
2 tablespoons water
2 oz. sugar
2 tablespoons chopped onions

5 crushed peppercorns
10 crushed allspice
2 sprigs fresh dill
sliced onion and chopped
dill for garnish

Wash, clean and fillet herring. Then soak in cold water for about 12 hours. Remove skin and any bones that may be left. Dry carefully and slice diagonally into ¼-inch or ½-inch pieces, using very sharp knife. Arrange neatly in serving dish. This is best done by sliding knife under herring and lifting all at once. Mix all ingredients (except garnish) in saucepan, bring to the boil and simmer for 5 minutes. Set to cool, strain and pour over herring. Garnish with dill and onion rings, cover and chill overnight. Serve on smorgasbord with small boiled potatoes.

SOUR HERRING

Norwegian

6 SERVINGS

3 salted herring fillets	$\frac{1}{2}$ pint vinegar
2 large onions	$\frac{1}{4}$ pint water

Soak salted herrings in cold water for 12 hours. Dry them and remove skins. Cut into little strips. Slice onions. Place alternate layers of herring and onions in a glass jar. Mix water and vinegar and pour over, so that the herring is completely covered. The exact quantity needed depends on the size of the jar, but the proportion should be 2 to 1. Stand in a cool place for at least 12 hours, but it can be kept for up to 2 weeks. When serving, take herring out of vinegar and garnish with a little onion, freshly sliced. Sometimes a little freshly ground pepper is added on top.

SPRATS IN TOMATO SAUCE

Swedish

4 SERVINGS

1 lb. sprats	2 tablespoons tomato purée
6 tablespoons oil	sugar
2 tablespoons vinegar	salt and pepper

Clean the fish and wash carefully. Soak in cold, salted water (3 tablespoons salt to 2 pints water) for a few minutes. Remove fish, drain well and discard water. Place fish close together in a saucepan with backs uppermost. Mix other ingredients well, using salt, pepper and sugar to taste. Pour the sauce over fish and poach for 7—8 minutes. Remove fish carefully, taking care that they do not fall apart, and place in a suitable serving dish. Pour sauce over and cool. Serve well chilled at the smorgasbord.

MARINATED SPRATS

Swedish

4 SERVINGS

1½ lb. sprats	½ tablespoon sugar
2 tablespoons chopped fresh dill	5 tablespoons oil
½ tablespoon salt	½ teaspoon pepper
1 teaspoon French mustard	2 tablespoons vinegar

Clean sprats and wash them carefully. Open and remove bone. Skin and soak for a few minutes in cold, salted water (3 tablespoons salt to 2 pints water). Remove and dry well, discarding water. Place a little chopped dill in the bottom of a bowl. Put in sprats and rest of dill in layers. Mix other ingredients together and pour over fish. Take a fork and lift up layers of sprats a little so that marinade can penetrate. Let it stand in a cold place for 3 hours. Chill well before placing on a serving dish, garnish with sprigs of dill and serve at the smorgasbord.

This dish can also be made with fresh mackerel, in which case mackerel fillets are sliced thinly, slant-wise towards the skin.

BUCKLING IN SALAD SAUCE

Swedish

4 SERVINGS

6 smoked bucklings	1 tablespoon vinegar
2 tablespoons chopped dill	3 tablespoons oil
2 tablespoons chopped chives	salt and pepper

Clean and fillet fish, removing all skin and bones. Divide in nice pieces and arrange neatly in serving dish. Sprinkle with chopped chives and dill. Mix oil and vinegar carefully and season to taste with salt and pepper. Pour over fish, chill a little and serve.

MACKEREL FOR THE SMORGASBORD

Swedish

4 SERVINGS

2 lb. mackerel	5 tablespoons mayonnaise
1 tablespoon salt	5 tablespoons whipped cream
2 tablespoons vinegar	2 tablespoons chopped dill
10 white peppercorns	2 tablespoons chopped parsley
¼ lemon	2 tablespoons chopped chives
1 onion	2 hard-boiled eggs
sprigs of dill	2 tomatoes
lettuce	

Clean the mackerel and place in a fish kettle with sufficient water to cover. Add salt, vinegar, peppercorns, lemon, onion and a few sprigs of dill. Bring to boil and simmer for about 15 minutes, when meat should come free from the bone. Let it cool in the stock overnight. Shortly before serving, mackerel should be filleted and skin removed. Arrange some lettuce leaves on a serving dish and place filleted mackerel on top. Mix mayonnaise and cream and spread over mackerel. Mix chopped parsley, dill and chives and sprinkle on top. Quarter eggs and tomatoes and arrange nicely around fish. Serve on smorgasbord with little, new, boiled potatoes.

MARINATED SALMON

Swedish

8 SERVINGS

2 lb. fresh salmon   20 white peppercorns
5 oz. salt   fresh dill
3 oz. sugar

Prepare piece of salmon in fillets, removing bone but leaving the skin on. Do not wash unless necessary, in which case it should be washed quickly and then dried by wrapping in a clean cloth. Place a thick layer of fresh dill in a deep bowl. Crush peppercorns and mix with salt and sugar. Rub salmon with some of this mixture, and sprinkle some on top of the dill. Place one fillet with skin side down on top of dill. Place a layer of dill on top and sprinkle some salt mixture on it. Place other fillet on top, skin side up, so that the thicker part of one fillet meets the thinner part of the other. Place another layer of dill on this and sprinkle rest of salt mixture over it. Cover fish with a plate that fits upside down into the bowl, and place something heavy on it so that fish is pressed down. Stand in a cool place for 6—24 hours, during which time fish should be turned over a few times in a body, without disturbing the layers. When ready to be served, scrape off seasoning, slice slantwise towards the skin, place on a cold serving dish and garnish with sprigs of fresh dill.

EGGS STUFFED WITH TUNA FISH

Danish

hard-boiled eggs mayonnaise
tuna fish lettuce

Peel eggs and cut in halves. Mix egg yolks with equal amount
of tinned tuna fish. Heap this into egg halves. Top with
teaspoon mayonnaise and place on dish decorated with
lettuce leaves. Serve on smorgasbord.

EGGS IN MAYONNAISE

Danish

hard-boiled eggs paprika
mayonnaise lettuce

Peel hard-boiled eggs and cut in halves. Wash and drain
small lettuce leaves. Put 1 teaspoon mayonnaise on each leaf
and stand 1 egg half, with yolk down, in mayonnaise. Top
with 2 teaspoons mayonnaise and sprinkle with paprika.
Arrange close together on dish and serve on smorgasbord.

STUFFED EGGS WITH CURRY

Danish

hard-boiled eggs lettuce
curry powder salt
mayonnaise

Peel hard-boiled eggs and cut in halves. Remove yolk and
mix with mayonnaise and curry powder to taste. Season

with salt. Wash lettuce leaves and drain well. Spread leaves over a serving dish. Stuff egg halves with mixture so that they are piled high and arrange decoratively on dish.

EGGS STUFFED WITH SARDINES

Danish

hard-boiled eggs
sardines in oil
mayonnaise

French mustard
lettuce

Wash and drain lettuce. Spread leaves over serving dish. Shell eggs and cut in halves. Mix egg yolks with equal amount of boned, drained sardines. Stir in mayonnaise and a little French mustard to taste, blending until smooth. Pile high in egg halves, place on lettuce and serve on smorgasbord.

EGG AND TOMATO 'MUSHROOMS'

Norwegian

4 SERVINGS

4 hard-boiled eggs
4 small firm tomatoes

salt and pepper

Slice off a little of the broader end of eggs and stand them up. Cut off top of each tomato and remove about a teaspoon of the pulp. Sprinkle inside of tomato with salt and pepper to taste. Fit each tomato on top of an egg, so that they look like red and white mushrooms. Serve on smorgasbord with mayonnaise, which looks nice placed in a small bowl in centre of the dish, surrounded by 'mushrooms'.

STUFFED EGG

Norwegian

2 SERVINGS

8 peeled shrimps	1 anchovy fillet
1 hard-boiled egg	1 teaspoon butter

Cut egg carefully in half. Cut a thin slice off the end of each half, so that egg halves will stand up. Remove yolk and pound it together with butter and anchovy until it is well mixed and smooth. Place 4 shrimps on edge of each egg white, so that they curve outwards. Fill centres with yolk mixture. Chop the slice of egg white and sprinkle on top. Serve on smorgasbord with mayonnaise.

BIRD'S NEST

Swedish

2 SERVINGS

12 anchovy fillets	chopped chives
2 raw egg yolks	chopped pickled beetroot
2 tablespoons chopped	chopped cold boiled
raw onion	potatoes
capers	

Place in 2 circles piles of chopped anchovy, capers, chopped chives, chopped beetroot and chopped cold boiled potatoes. Place a raw egg yolk carefully in the centre of each circle. Season with very little salt and freshly ground pepper to taste. Chill and serve on smorgasbord.

ANCHOVY EYE

Swedish

4 SERVINGS

8 anchovy fillets 1 raw egg yolk
½ medium onion

Chop raw onion finely and place in a ring on a small plate.
Chop anchovy fillets and place in a ring around onion. Place
raw egg yolk in the centre. Chill well and serve with smorgasbord. This dish looks attractive on the table, and is quite
delicious to the connoisseur. (The ingredients should be
mixed together before being eaten.)

MEATBALLS FOR SMORGASBORD

Swedish

4 SERVINGS

1 lb. minced beef   2 teaspoons salt
1 oz. butter   ¼ teaspoon pepper
3 tablespoons chopped onion 1 carton single cream
4 tablespoons breadcrumbs   (2·7 fluid oz.)
¼ pint water   margarine for frying

Place breadcrumbs in large mixing bowl, add cream and
water. Let stand to swell. Fry finely chopped onions in
butter until golden brown and add to bowl. Mix in meat,
stirring very well until smooth and creamy in texture. Stir
in seasoning. Form mixture into small round balls ¾ inch
in diameter and fry in margarine until evenly brown. This
is best achieved by gently shaking pan, so that meat balls
roll, which also helps to maintain their shape. Serve cold
on smorgasbord.

RAW BEEF

Swedish

4 SERVINGS

1 lb. fillet steak	1 large boiled beetroot
4 egg yolks	1 tablespoon vinegar
2 medium onions	salt and pepper

Mince fillet steak finely and form into 4 cakes. Season with salt and a generous amount of freshly ground pepper. Place on serving dish. Chop beetroot finely and soak in vinegar for 30 minutes. Drain and place on serving dish and make 4 piles. Chop onion finely and place in 4 piles on serving dish. Place the raw egg yolks in their halved egg shells in the centre of the dish. Serve chilled on smorgasbord. This dish can also be arranged to form 4 eyes, in which case egg yolks are placed in the middle, each one surrounded by rings of steak, onion and beetroot.

HERRING SALAD

Norwegian

10 SERVINGS

1 lb. salted herring fillets	1 lb. cooked veal
1 lb. boiled potatoes	1 lb. boiled beetroots
1 lb. raw cooking apples	1 small pickled cucumber
4 tablespoons oil	4 tablespoons vinegar
2 tablespoons claret	sugar to taste
salt and pepper	1 hard-boiled egg for garnish

Soak herring fillets in cold water for 6 hours. Dry them, remove skin and cut into little cubes. Cut all other solid ingredients in little cubes and mix them all together in a bowl. Mix 2 tablespoons oil, 2 tablespoons vinegar, claret and a little sugar and pour over the salad. Stand in a cool place overnight. Put the rest of the oil and vinegar in a small bowl. Place this in boiling water and stir continuously until sauce thickens. Season with salt and pepper to taste. Let it cool. Spread this sauce over top of salad. Chop hard-boiled egg finely and use as garnish. Serve on the smorgasbord.

HERRING SALAD (I)

Swedish

4—6 SERVINGS

2 salt herring fillets	1 large apple
5 medium cold boiled potatoes	1 teaspoon chopped onion
	5 tablespoons vinegar
5 medium cold boiled beetroots	$\frac{1}{4}$ teaspoon pepper
	1 hard-boiled egg
1 medium gherkin	parsley

Mix vinegar, pepper and chopped onion in a bowl. Cut herring, potatoes, beetroots, gherkin and apple into $\frac{1}{4}$-inch cubes and add to the bowl, mixing carefully with 2 forks. Put salad in a serving dish and press down the top so that the surface is even. Chill for 30 minutes. Decorate with egg white, egg yolk and parsley, chopped separately, by making stripes or checks on top of salad. Serve salad with strong sauce (see page 72) or sour cream.

2 tins anchovy fillets can be substituted for the herring.

HERRING SALAD (II)

Swedish

4 SERVINGS

2 salt herring fillets
3 medium cold boiled
  potatoes
2 hard-boiled eggs
1 carton double cream
  (2·7 fluid oz.)
salt and pepper

½ portion mayonnaise
  (see page 73)
½ tablespoon vinegar
1½ tablespoons oil

Mix oil and vinegar in a bowl. Cut herring, potatoes and egg whites into ¼-inch cubes and add them to the bowl. Stir carefully, using 2 forks. Chill for 30 minutes. Beat cream until it is thick and stir in mayonnaise. Mix salad with two-thirds of the sauce. Season to taste. Spread the washed and well drained lettuce leaves on a serving dish. Pile salad on top and pour rest of sauce over it. Chop egg yolks finely and sprinkle on top.

SHRIMP SALAD

Swedish

4 SERVINGS

1 lb. peeled shrimps
2 celery stalks

lettuce
mayonnaise

Clean and scrape celery. Cut it across in thin slices. Place shrimps and celery in a bowl. Stir in mayonnaise (half the quantity suggested on page 73). Chill for 30 minutes.

Rinse lettuce leaves and drain carefully. Spread lettuce leaves on a serving dish and pile salad on top.

This can be made equally well with lobster, crab or tinned mussels.

FISH SALAD

Swedish

4 SERVINGS

10 oz. boiled boned fish
1 small tin asparagus
   tips or peas
1 hard-boiled egg

1 firm tomato
strong fish sauce
   (page 72)
lettuce

When fish is cold separate it into nice pieces and make sure no bones remain. Drain vegetable well and add to the fish. Stir in half the strong sauce. Spread washed and well drained lettuce leaves on a serving dish and pile fish salad on top. Pour rest of sauce on top. Slice tomato and egg and place it around salad as garnish.

MOCK LOBSTER COCKTAIL

Norwegian

4 SERVINGS

6 oz. boiled white fish
2 oz. shrimps, peeled
1 medium celeriac
(or 1 cup diced celery)
2 tablespoons oil
1 tablespoon vinegar

1 teaspoon salt
½ teaspoon pepper
1 tablespoon chopped
parsley
lobster colouring
lettuce leaves

Bone the fish carefully and divide into nice pieces. Scrub the celeriac and boil it, peel and cut into small dice. Mix the fish and diced celeriac carefully, using 2 forks. Make a salad dressing of oil, vinegar and spices and pour over slowly whilst mixing the salad. Sprinkle parsley over it, add the colouring and mix all together. Place lettuce leaves in cocktail glasses and heap the salad on top. Decorate with shrimps and serve chilled.

SHRIMP SALAD

Norwegian

6 SERVINGS

6 oz. peeled shrimps
1 small tin fine peas
3 tablespoons diced
cucumber
6 tablespoons mayonnaise
3 tablespoons whipped cream

1 hard-boiled egg
2 tomatoes
2 tablespoons chopped
parsley
lettuce leaves
salt and pepper

Mix the shrimps, cucumber and well drained peas together and season to taste. Mix cream and mayonnaise and stir carefully into the salad. Spread the lettuce leaves on a serving dish and heap salad on top. Chop hard-boiled egg finely and sprinkle over salad, together with chopped parsley. Quarter the tomatoes and place decoratively around the salad. Serve chilled.

BIRGITTE SALAD

Norwegian

4—6 SERVINGS

8 oz. boiled white fish
4 oz. boiled peas
4 oz. raw grated carrots
1 grated apple
1 orange
2 gherkins
2 tablespoons vinegar

2 tablespoons oil
3 tablespoons water
3 tablespoons sugar
½ teaspoon salt
pepper or paprika to
  taste
lettuce leaves

Bone the fish carefully and divide into nice pieces. Chop gherkins and cut up orange finely. Mix the fish and vegetables carefully in a bowl, using 2 forks. Mix all other ingredients into a sauce and pour over the salad. Spread lettuce leaves over a serving dish and pile the salad on top.

FISH SALAD WITH MACARONI AND PEAS

Norwegian

4—6 SERVINGS

8 oz. boiled white fish	4 tablespoons chopped
4 oz. boiled peas	gherkins
4 oz. boiled macaroni	mayonnaise (see page 73)
	lettuce and sliced tomato

Bone the fish carefully and divide into nice pieces. Put in a bowl with macaroni, peas and chopped gherkins. Pour mayonnaise over and mix it all carefully, using 2 forks. Garnish a serving dish with lettuce leaves, spreading them over the whole plate. Heap the salad in the middle of the plate and place sliced tomatoes around it.

FISH SALAD WITH HORSERADISH SAUCE

Norwegian

4—6 SERVINGS

8 oz. boiled white fish	2 tablespoons freshly
3 tomatoes	grated horse-radish
1 lettuce	2 hard-boiled eggs
1 carton sour cream	salt and pepper
(5 fluid oz.)	

Bone the fish carefully and divide into nice pieces. Cut tomatoes into fairly small pieces. Wash and drain the lettuce and cut it into strips. Mix the fish, tomatoes and lettuce in a salad bowl. Beat the sour cream until smooth and stir in grated horse-radish. Season with salt and pepper. Mix this sauce carefully into the salad. Garnish with the hard-boiled eggs cut into quarters.

FISH SALAD WITH MUSTARD SAUCE

Norwegian

4—6 SERVINGS

8 oz. boiled white fish
4 oz. chopped celery
4 oz. chopped apples
2 tablespoons lemon juice
2 tablespoons margarine
1 tablespoon flour
1 tablespoon vinegar

2 tablespoons water
3 tablespoons sugar
2 tablespoons French
  mustard
1 egg
1 carton double cream
  (2·7 fluid oz.)
lettuce leaves

Bone the fish carefully and divide into nice pieces. Place in a bowl and mix carefully with apples and celery, using 2 forks to prevent it from getting mushy. Decorate a plate with salad leaves and heap the salad on it. Pour lemon juice over salad. The sauce should be prepared in advance in the following manner. Melt the butter in a saucepan and stir in flour. Then stir in vinegar, water, sugar and mustard, letting it simmer on a low flame. Beat the egg and stir in last. Let it thicken without coming to the boil. Remove from heat and set to cool. Then stir in whipped cream. Chill and pour over the fish salad before serving.

BUCKLING SALAD WITH MAYONNAISE

Swedish

4 SERVINGS

6 smoked bucklings
6 tablespoons mayonnaise
3 tablespoons double cream
1 tablespoon chopped chives
1 hard-boiled egg

2 tablespoons chopped onion
2 tablespoons chopped apple
2 tablespoons chopped pickled beetroot

Clean and fillet fish, removing all skin and bones. Divide into nice pieces and arrange neatly on serving dish. Mix mayonnaise with cream and cover fish with it. Sprinkle with chopped chives. Place piles of chopped onion, beetroot, apple, chopped egg white, chopped yolk around the fish in decorative manner. Chill a little and serve.

FRANKFURTER SALAD

Swedish

4 SERVINGS

6 medium potatoes
3 Frankfurters
2 tablespoons capers
1 tablespoon vinegar
3 tablespoons oil

3 tablespoons tomato juice
1 teaspoon grated onion
$\frac{1}{2}$ teaspoon salt
pepper

Boil potatoes in their skins. Test with a fork to see they are done. Pour off water and hold pot over flame to dry them a little. Place in dish and cool. Peel and cut into $\frac{1}{2}$ inch cubes. Peel Frankfurters and cut into $\frac{1}{4}$ inch slices. Mix vinegar, oil, tomato juice, grated onion, salt and pepper in a salad bowl. Add potatoes, Frankfurters and capers.

Stir well and season with additional pepper to taste. Chill for 30 minutes, stir again and serve.

MOTHER'S MEAT SALAD

Danish

4 SERVINGS

1 cup diced meat (any left-over roast)
2 cups diced boiled potatoes
1 medium onion, chopped

4 tablespoons oil
1 tablespoon vinegar
salt and pepper
1 tablespoon chopped parsley

Mix oil and vinegar in salad bowl. Stir in meat, potatoes and onion. Season to taste with salt and pepper. Sprinkle parsley on top.

RAW VEGETABLE SALAD

Swedish

6 SERVINGS

8 tablespoons grated carrots
8 tablespoons grated beetroot
8 tablespoons shredded cabbage
8 tablespoons shredded leek
¼ cucumber
3 tomatoes

2 tablespoons chopped parsley
3 tablespoons lemon juice
6 tablespoons oil
sugar
salt and pepper

Arrange the grated and shredded vegetables on a large dish in piles, so that the colours make a pretty combination. The piles should be close together without mixing. Slice tomatoes and cucumber and place decoratively around vegetables. Sprinkle with parsley. Mix in oil and lemon juice well and season to taste with salt, pepper and sugar. Pour over the salad and chill for 5 minutes. Serve with mayonnaise.

AUTUMN SALAD

Swedish

4 SERVINGS

1 large lettuce
2 apples
1 lb. plums
2 tablespoons chopped nuts
lemon juice

3 tablespoons boiled diced
  celeriac
4 tablespoons mayonnaise
3 tablespoons double cream

Wash and drain lettuce. Peel, core and dice apples. Sprinkle a little lemon juice over apples to prevent them from turning brown. Pour boiling water over plums, peel, cut in two and remove stones. Stir in mayonnaise and cream. Mix all ingredients apart from lettuce by turning gently with 2 forks. Spread lettuce over large dish or bowl and pile salad in centre. Chill and serve with cold meat.

MIXED VEGETABLE SALAD

Danish

4 SERVINGS

1 large celeriac
2 pickled beetroots

2 cooking apples
5 tablespoons mayonnaise

Peel and dice celeriac and apples. Dice beetroots. There should be about equal quantities of each. Place in salad bowl and stir in mayonnaise. Serve immediately.

MIXED SALAD

Swedish

6—8 SERVINGS

3 oz. salted boiled tongue	2 medium boiled carrots
3 oz. boiled ham	½ gherkin
2 apples	12 tablespoons mayonnaise
8 oz. frozen peas	¼ pint double cream
4 medium boiled potatoes	lettuce, tomatoes, cucumber

Dice meat, apples, potatoes, carrots, gherkin and mix in bowl with de-frosted and drained peas. Mix mayonnaise with cream and carefully stir into salad, using 2 forks. Chill and serve on lettuce leaves and garnish with tomatoes and cucumber. This salad can also be used for stuffing raw tomatoes.

CHICKEN SALAD

Danish

4 SERVINGS

cold diced chicken (about 1½ cups)	1 tablespoon grated horse-radish
3 hard-boiled eggs	5 tablespoons whipped cream
1 tablespoon vinegar	1 tablespoon chopped parsley
	salt and pepper

Mash 3 hard-boiled eggs and mix in horseradish and vinegar. Stir in whipped cream. Mix in diced chicken. Season to taste with salt and pepper. Place in salad bowl and sprinkle parsley on top.

CHRISTMAS SALAD

Danish

4 SERVINGS

2 endives
2 pickled beetroots
2 cooking apples

5 tablespoons mayonnaise
1—2 teaspoons vinegar
   from beetroots

Peel and dice apples, cut up beetroots and endives. There should be about equal quantities of each. Mix the mayonnaise with vinegar from the beetroots, adjusting the quantity according to taste. Place vegetables in salad bowl and stir in dressing. Serve immediately.

GRANDMOTHER'S SALAD

Danish

6 SERVINGS

8 oz. macaroni
8 oz. lean ham
2 eggs

$\frac{1}{2}$ teaspoon salt
1 teaspoon mustard powder
$\frac{1}{2}$ pint sour cream

Boil macaroni in salted water and rinse in cold water until cool. Drain well. Boil eggs 7 minutes and let cool in cold water. Mince or chop ham. Peel eggs and remove yolks, which should be not quite hard boiled. Mix egg yolks with salt and mustard powder by mashing with a fork. When smooth mix with sour cream. Chop egg whites and mix with equal part of minced ham. In a salad bowl place layers of macaroni, sour cream mixture and minced ham. For top layer use egg white and ham mixture. Serve on smorgasbord.

MACARONI SALAD

Danish

4 SERVINGS

8 oz. mixed carrots
 and peas, tinned
4 oz. macaroni

6 tablespoons mayonnaise
salt and pepper

Boil macaroni in salted water and rinse in cold water until cool. Drain well. Mix with diced vegetables. Stir in mayonnaise and season with salt and pepper to taste.

CABBAGE AND APPLE SALAD

Swedish

4 SERVINGS

10 oz. shredded white
 cabbage
2 apples

juice of 1 orange
¼ pint double cream
sugar

Wash apples but do not peel them. Shred coarsely and mix with shredded cabbage. Mix cream and orange juice, adding a little sugar to taste. Pour over salad and serve chilled.

RED COLE SLAW

Danish

4 SERVINGS

red cabbage
vinegar

oil

Shred tender leaves of red cabbage. Place in bowl and cover with boiling water to which 2 tablespoons vinegar has been added. Soak for 1 hour. Drain well and mix with salad dressing made with 3 parts oil to 1 part vinegar.

CELERIAC SALAD

Danish

4 SERVINGS

2 celeriac
6 tablespoons mayonnaise
1 teaspoon French mustard

1 teaspoon chopped chives
1 teaspoon chopped parsley
salt, pepper and lemon juice

Scrub celeriac and boil in salted water until soft. Drain, peel, dice and set to cool. Mix mayonnaise with mustard, chives and parsley. Turn celeriac gently in this dressing and season to taste with salt, pepper and lemon juice.

SAUERKRAUT SALAD

Danish

4 SERVINGS

4 medium boiled potatoes
1 large boiled beetroot
4 oz. sauerkraut
1½ gherkins

1 medium onion
4 tablespoons oil
1½ tablespoons vinegar
salt and pepper

Mix oil and vinegar in salad bowl. Stir in diced potatoes and beetroot. Chop onion and gherkins and add. Drain sauerkraut well and mix with the rest. Season to taste with salt and pepper.

WHITE COLE SLAW

Danish

4 SERVINGS

white cabbage	chopped parsley
oil	chopped chives
vinegar	salt and pepper

Remove coarse leaves and stalks from cabbage. Shred it finely. Make salad dressing with 3 parts oil to 1 part vinegar. Season to taste with salt and pepper. Mix cabbage well with generous amount of dressing. Let it stand 2 hours. Sprinkle with equal amounts chopped chives and parsley and serve.

CUCUMBER SALAD

Swedish

4 SERVINGS

½ cucumber	sugar
1 tablespoon vinegar	salt and pepper
1 tablespoon oil	

Peel cucumber and slice very thinly over a plate. Sprinkle a little salt between layers. Place another plate on top so that it presses down and stand for 1 hour. Pour off juice that has collected. Mix oil and vinegar and add a pinch of sugar and pepper to taste. Place cucumbers in a salad dish and mix in the dressing by turning the slices. Serve on the smorgasbord. This salad is also served as a relish with roasts.

FRENCH BEANS AND TOMATO SALAD

Danish

4 SERVINGS

8 oz. frozen or fresh
  French beans
8 oz. firm tomatoes
2 tablespoons chopped
  onions

2 tablespoons chopped
  parsley
3 tablespoons oil
3 tablespoons vinegar
salt and pepper

De-frost and boil beans in salted water. Set to cool in water. Drain very well. Make a bed of beans in a salad bowl, but if they are long it is better to cut them into 1½ inch strips. Slice tomatoes quite thinly, but so that each slice holds together. Spread slices over bean bed. Sprinkle chopped onions on top, and finally chopped parsley. Mix oil and vinegar well and season to taste with salt and pepper. Pour dressing over salad and serve.

POTATO AND TOMATO SALAD

Danish

boiled potatoes
firm tomatoes
mayonnaise

chopped chives
salt and pepper

Slice equal amounts of cold boiled potatoes and tomatoes into pieces thick enough to hold together. Sprinkle with a little salt and pepper. Dip each slice in mayonnaise and place alternately in overlapping rows. Sprinkle with chopped chives.

POTATO SALAD

Swedish

4 SERVINGS

8 medium potatoes
1 medium onion
2 tablespoons vinegar
6 tablespoons oil
1 teaspoon salt

freshly ground pepper
2 teaspoons chopped
parsley
1 teaspoon chopped chives
(celery)

Boil potatoes in their skins. Test with a fork to see they are done. Pour off water and hold pot over flame to dry them a little. Place in dish and cool. Peel and cut into $\frac{1}{2}$ inch cubes. Mix vinegar, oil, salt and pepper in a salad bowl. Chop onion finely and stir into salad sauce. Add potatoes and stir well. Let the salad stand for 30 minutes, stirring occasionally so that sauce is absorbed by potatoes. When ready to serve, mix in chopped chives and parsley and add a little fresh pepper to taste.

Chopped celery makes an interesting addition to this salad, in which case a larger quantity of salad dressing should be made, according to the amount of celery. The salad should be moist from the dressing to be at its best.

SIMPLE FISH SALAD

Norwegian

4 SERVINGS

left-over fish	1 tablespoon vinegar
1 lettuce	1 tablespoon sugar
3 tablespoons oil	pepper and salt

Bone fish carefully and cut into nice pieces. Wash lettuce, drain well and cut into strips. Mix fish and lettuce together. Make a salad dressing with oil, vinegar, sugar, salt and pepper. Pour over the salad and let it stand for a while. Decorate with some extra lettuce leaves.

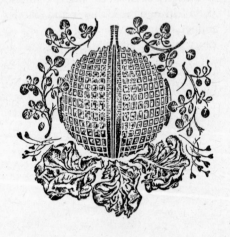

The open sandwich is of Danish origin but it has long been popular all over Scandinavia. If you want to do justice to it you must be generous with the ingredients, so that it is almost a meal in itself. It should also have visual appeal, and therefore great care should be taken in arranging and decorating it artistic-ally. The sandwich is often served as a snack in the evening, but it can also be taken as an appetizer instead of an hors-d'oeuvre. It is important to select the right bread for each combination of ingredients, and to spread the butter evenly to cover the entire sandwich. If the ingredients are moist, one must always place them on a lettuce leaf to prevent the bread from getting soggy. There are endless variations, but I have tried to select those which are the least complicated and requiring those ingredients readily available outside Scandinavia.

SANDWICH WITH CHEESE BUTTER

Danish

Danish Blue cheese   white bread
stuffed green olives   butter

Mix equal quantities of butter and cheese to a smooth paste, using a fork. Spread generous layer on each slice of bread. Remove crusts and cut slices into triangles or rectangles. Slice the olives so that each piece has pimento in the centre and decorate each sandwich with 3 such slices.

SANDWICH WITH BOILED FISH AND MAYONNAISE

Danish

boiled fish   white bread
lettuce   capers
mayonnaise   salt and pepper

Wash lettuce, drain and dry well. Butter the bread, remove crusts and cut into triangles. Place a small curved lettuce leaf on each piece. Bone cold fish carefully and cut into neat pieces. Put pieces of fish on each lettuce leaf. Season with salt and pepper to taste. Put a generous amount of mayonnaise over fish. Garnish with a few capers.

SANDWICH WITH CHEESE AND RADISHES

Danish

sliced cheese   brown bread
radishes   butter

Butter bread and remove crusts. Wash radishes and slice thinly. Cover bread entirely with cheese. Put rows of overlapping radish slices on the cheese, making a nice design.

STRIP SANDWICH
WITH DANISH BLUE CHEESE

Danish

Danish Blue cheese   butter
thinly sliced pumpernickel

Mix equal quantities of butter and Danish Blue cheese to smooth paste, using a fork. Spread 3 slices pumpernickel generously with cheese mixture. Place slices on top of each other. Cover this with another slice of pumpernickel. Cut this pile in strips about 1 inch wide, using very sharp knife. Each pile will make 4 strips of sandwiches.

SMOKED FISH SANDWICH

Danish

smoked fish   lettuce
bread slices   butter
hard-boiled egg   mayonnaise

Toast bread and butter it. Cover each piece with a well washed and dried lettuce leaf. Bone the fish and remove skin. Divide it into strips. Place a strip of fish in centre of each sandwich, running from end to end. Chop hard-boiled egg and place in a strip on either side. Decorate with mayonnaise.

MIXED CHEESE SANDWICH

Danish

Danish Blue cheese   butter
Petit Suisse cheese   parsley
thinly sliced pumpernickel

Mix equal quantities of Danish Blue cheese, Petit Suisse
cheese and butter to a smooth paste. Spread pumpernickel
slices generously with this. Sprinkle with chopped parsley
and cut into shapes, for example triangles, etc.

CREAM CHEESE SANDWICH

Danish

cream cheese   cucumber
pumpernickel   radishes
butter

Butter the pumpernickel and spread generously with cream
cheese. Slice cucumber and radishes thinly. Place an overlapping row of cucumber in middle of each sandwich and
a row of overlapping radish slices on either side.

SANDWICH WITH CHEESE, SHRIMPS
AND MAYONNAISE

Danish

shrimps, peeled   white bread
sliced cheese   butter
mayonnaise   parsley

Butter the bread and remove crusts. Cut cheese into strips
and place 3 on each piece of bread, running from edge to

edge. Place 2 rows of shrimps between cheese strips. Place dabs of mayonnaise on the shrimps and decorate with small sprigs of parsley.

SANDWICH WITH MIXED VEGETABLES AND MAYONNAISE

Danish

tinned mixed vegetables	parsley
bread to choice	lettuce
mayonnaise	salt and pepper
butter	

Butter bread and remove crusts. Drain vegetables well. Wash and dry lettuce. Place a small curved lettuce leaf on each piece of bread. Put a pile of vegetables on each lettuce leaf. Season with a little salt and generous amount of pepper, preferably freshly ground. Put generous amount of mayonnaise over vegetables. Garnish with a little chopped parsley.

SALMON BUTTER AND ASPARAGUS SANDWICH

Danish

2 oz. smoked salmon	white bread
3 oz. butter	pepper
tinned asparagus tips	

Remove crusts of bread and cut each slice in half so that rectangles remain. Chop salmon finely. Pass salmon and butter through a fine sieve, using a wooden spoon. Season with pepper to taste. Spread salmon butter fairly generously on bread. Let asparagus drain well and place one piece lengthwise on each sandwich.

SARDINE SANDWICH ON EGG
AND ONION BED

Danish

hard-boiled eggs   white bread
raw onion   butter
sardines in oil

Butter bread and remove crusts. Chop egg whites and yolks
separately. Chop onion finely. Put strips of egg white, onion
and yolk across bread. Drain sardines so that they are not
too oily. Place 1 sardine across the strips on each sandwich.

ANCHOVY AND CHOPPED EGG SANDWICH

Danish

anchovy   butter
hard-boiled eggs   capers
dark bread

About 1 egg and 4 fillets of anchovy will be needed for each
slice of bread.
Butter bread and remove crusts so that a square remains.
Chop egg whites and yolks separately and finely. Place
anchovy in squares or strips across the bread. Fill in spaces
with alternating egg white and yolk, so that it makes a nice
design. Dot the chopped egg with capers.

SANDWICH WITH SMOKED SALMON AND EGG

Danish

smoked salmon   butter
hard-boiled egg   fresh dill
white bread

Cut each slice of bread into a nice round shape, removing

edges. Butter each slice and cover neatly with smoked salmon, cut to size. Slice hard-boiled egg and place one piece in centre of each sandwich. Garnish with a small sprig of dill.

HERRING SANDWICH

Danish

tinned herring *(gaffelbitar)*   sour cream
rye bread   chopped chives
lettuce   butter

Sliced rye bread will do well for this sandwich. Butter each slice carefully. Cover it with a washed and dried lettuce leaf. Place a row of herring pieces diagonally across the sandwich. Put a teaspoon of whipped sour cream in the other two corners. Sprinkle all over with chopped chives.

SANDWICH WITH SHELLFISH AND MAYONNAISE

Danish

tinned shellfish to choice   white bread
fresh dill   butter
mayonnaise   lettuce

Wash lettuce, drain and dry well. Butter each slice of bread. Place a lettuce leaf on top and press down so that it lies flat. Cut off crusts of bread so that neat squares remain. Place shellfish on top in a nice design. Decorate with mayonnaise and small sprigs of dill.

SMOKED EEL SANDWICH

Danish

smoked eel   lettuce
toast   butter
cold scrambled egg

Make toast and spread with butter. Cover each sandwich with a well washed and dried lettuce leaf. Fillet the eel, removing skin and all the bones. Divide meat into strips. Place a strip of eel in centre of each sandwich, running from edge to edge. Pile a row of scrambled egg on either side.

POULTRY SANDWICH

Danish

cold cooked poultry lettuce
white bread   mayonnaise

Butter the bread and cover each slice with a well washed and dried lettuce leaf. The poultry should be boned and neatly sliced. Place a generous portion on each sandwich and decorate with mayonnaise.

SALT BEEF SANDWICH

Danish

sliced salt beef French mustard
rye bread   butter
gherkins

Mix 1 teaspoon French mustard with each 2 oz. butter. Spread on each slice of bread. Cover the entire sandwich with slices of salt beef. Slice gherkins thinly crosswise and place an overlapping row of gherkin slices diagonally across the sandwich.

Some soups in this section are almost a meal in themselves, an approach to this food which is typically Scandinavian. It is, for example, traditional in Sweden to serve pea soup with bacon every Thursday, followed by pancakes and cranberries. This makes a very tasty and satisfying meal. It is worth trying, though you probably need to be brought up with it to appreciate having it on your menu every week!

Other recipes are not dissimilar to the sort of soup eaten in England or France, but the slight variations to be found in Scandinavian soups will provide a change for those who consider themselves connoisseurs of this course.

TOMATO SOUP (1)

Swedish

4—5 SERVINGS

2 lb. soup bones	$\frac{1}{4}$ celeriac
2 lb. tomatoes	(or $\frac{1}{4}$ cup diced celery)
2$\frac{1}{2}$ pints water	4 potatoes
2 leeks	salt and pepper

Rinse bones and put to boil in cold water. Skim off any foam and season with salt and pepper. Clean leeks and slice them. Peel potatoes and celeriac and dice. Add these vegetables to soup and simmer for 1 hour. Cut up tomatoes and add to soup. Simmer for another 30 minutes. Remove bones and pass soup through sieve. Pour back into pot and bring to the boil again. Season to taste and serve.

TOMATO SOUP (2)

Swedish

4 SERVINGS

1 tin tomato paste (6 oz.)	1 tablespoon flour
1 tablespoon dripping	2$\frac{1}{4}$ pints water
4 slices bacon	1 bouillon cube
1 large chopped onion	2 tablespoons sour cream
2 sliced carrots	salt and pepper
2 tablespoons chopped parsley	

Melt dripping in large cast iron pot. Add onion, carrots and cut up bacon. Sauté for 5 minutes on low heat. Stir in flour and tomato paste. Gradually add water whilst stirring, then add bouillon cube. Stir until well blended and season to taste. Cover and simmer 30—40 minutes until carrots are tender. Remove from fire, stir in sour cream and chopped parsley.

TOMATO SOUP (3)

Swedish

5 SERVINGS

2½ lb. ripe tomatoes
1 pint chicken stock
2 tablespoons dripping
2 chopped onions
1 clove garlic
2 stalks celery

2 oz. butter
2 tablespoons flour
1 bouillon cube
2 tablespoons dry sherry
2 tablespoons chopped parsley
salt and pepper

Melt dripping in cast iron pot and sauté onion and garlic for 5 minutes. Wash tomatoes and celery, cut up and add to pot. Pour in stock and simmer, covered, for 40 minutes. Pass through fine sieve. Melt butter in pot and stir in flour. Add tomato purée and bouillon while stirring until well blended. Season to taste and stir in sherry. Sprinkle with chopped parsley and serve.

PEA SOUP WITH BACON

Swedish

4—6 SERVINGS

2 knuckles smoked bacon
1 lb. split peas
1 large onion

2 teaspoons thyme
3 pints water
pepper

Soak knuckles and peas separately overnight in sufficient water to cover well. Drain them, discarding water, and place all the ingredients in soup pot. Bring to the boil and simmer for about 3 hours, or until peas are soft and like a purée. Stir occasionally during this time and add a little extra water if necessary, depending on how thick a soup is desired. When the soup is ready, take out knuckles, remove skin and bones, cut up bacon and replace in soup. Season to taste and serve.

CAULIFLOWER SOUP

Swedish

4 SERVINGS

2 lb. cauliflower	2 egg yolks
1 pint stock	3 tablespoons single cream
1 pint water	2 tablespoons chopped parsley
2 oz. butter	salt and pepper

Wash cauliflower and break it into sections, removing tough stem. Place in a large saucepan with boiling water and 1 teaspoon salt, simmer until soft, about 15 minutes. Take a wire whisk and beat vigorously until cauliflower is minced. Add stock, bring to boil and season to taste with salt and pepper. Stir in butter. Beat egg yolks, cream and parsley, beat quickly into soup and remove from heat. Serve immediately.

LEEK AND POTATO SOUP

Swedish

4—5 SERVINGS

4 leeks	1½ pints water
5 small potatoes	1 pint milk
1 oz. butter	salt and pepper

Clean and slice leeks. Melt butter in saucepan and slowly simmer leeks in it. Peel and slice potatoes and add to leeks. Pour in water and simmer until potatoes are nearly done. Add seasonings and milk and simmer until potatoes are soft. The soup is now ready to be served.

BROWN CABBAGE SOUP

Danish

6 SERVINGS

4 pints beef stock   2 oz. butter
1 white cabbage   10 peppercorns
½ oz. sugar   salt

Cut cabbage into ¾ inch squares. Melt butter in cast iron frying pan, add sugar and brown cabbage slowly. This is best done by putting a little cabbage into the frying pan at a time and stirring to prevent it from burning. Put the browned cabbage into a large saucepan and pour on stock. Add peppercorns and simmer for 2 hours. Season to taste and serve.

SOUP WITH CABBAGE

Swedish

4 SERVINGS

2 pints beef stock   6 black peppercorns
1 lb. white cabbage   4 white peppercorns
2 oz. butter   salt

Cut cabbage into ½ inch squares and brown in butter. Add to beef stock, rinsing out frying pan with some of the stock. Add peppercorns and simmer until cabbage is tender. Season to taste. (A good addition to this soup is a few Frankfurters cut in ½-inch pieces.)

SPRING SOUP

Swedish

4—5 SERVINGS

5 new carrots	2 oz. butter
2 leeks	2½ pints water
6 oz. spinach	2 egg yolks
1 bunch radishes	6 tablespoons cream
2½ tablespoons flour	salt and pepper

Wash carrots, leeks, spinach and radishes. Melt butter in saucepan and add sliced leeks and carrots. Season with salt and pepper and simmer for 5 minutes. Add water and bring to the boil. Simmer for 10 minutes. Add chopped spinach and sliced radishes. Mix flour in a little cold water and add whilst stirring. Simmer until carrots are soft. Remove from heat, stir in yolks mixed with cream. Serve immediately with little cheese sandwiches, plain or toasted.

EASY VEGETABLE SOUP

Swedish

4—5 SERVINGS

2½ pints stock	¼ celeriac
4 carrots	3 oz. spinach
1 parsnip	1 bunch radishes
1 large leek	2 oz. butter
4 potatoes	salt and pepper

Wash and peel vegetables. Put stock on to boil. Grate carrots, parsnip, celeriac and potatoes coarsely and add to stock. Slice and add leek. Season to taste and simmer for 10 minutes. Then add chopped spinach and sliced radishes and simmer for another 3 minutes Add butter and serve with bread and cheese.

CLEAR VEGETABLE SOUP

Swedish

4—5 SERVINGS

2½ pints stock	1 leek
2 carrots	2 oz. butter
1 parsnip	3 lettuce leaves
1 stalk celery	salt and pepper

Clean and dice vegetables. Brown the butter in frying pan and add vegetables. Fry until slightly browned. Place in saucepan and rinse out frying pan with some stock. Pour all stock into saucepan and simmer until vegetables are soft. Season with salt and pepper to taste. Cut lettuce leaves into strips and add to soup just before serving.

VEAL AND PORK MEATBALLS FOR SOUP

Swedish

4 SERVINGS

4 oz. minced veal	1 tablespoon finely chopped
4 oz. minced pork	onion
2 tablespoons breadcrumbs	3 tablespoons single cream
1 teaspoon salt	pepper

Place meat, onion, breadcrumbs and salt in bowl and mix well, stirring with a wooden spoon. Gradually stir in cream and season with a little pepper. When smooth form into small balls, about ¾ inch in diameter. Simmer gently for 5 minutes in soup with which they are to be served, for example cabbage soup.

TUESDAY SOUP

Swedish

4—6 SERVINGS

1 lb. pickled pork	1 parsnip
2½ pints water	¼ swede
3 tablespoons barley	3 medium potatoes
½ celeriac	2½ tablespoons flour
1 large carrot	salt and pepper
¾ pint milk	

Rinse pork and place in water. Bring to the boil and skim off any foam. Simmer for 1½ hours. Clean vegetables and cut into pieces. Rinse barley in cold water and add to soup. Boil for about 10 minutes. Add vegetables and simmer for about 30 minutes, or until they are soft. Pour off stock and strain it. Put meat and vegetables to the side and re-heat stock. Stir milk and flour until smooth and add gradually to boiling stock. Cut up meat and place back in soup together with vegetables. Simmer for another 10 minutes, season to taste and serve.

FRESH BACON SOUP

Danish

6 SERVINGS

3 lb. piece fresh bacon	1 celeriac
5 pints water	2 carrots
2 tablespoons salt	6 peppercorns
1 medium white cabbage	2 tablespoons chopped parsley

Put bacon to boil in cold salted water. Skim off any foam, turn down heat, cover and simmer for 2 hours. Clean and peel vegetables. Cut cabbage into 8 pieces, slice carrots and dice celeriac. Add vegetables, peppercorns and parsley to soup. Bring to the boil again and simmer for 1 hour. Strain soup. Place vegetables in bottom of soup tureen and pour in soup. Slice bacon and serve separately, with soup.

LAMB AND VEGETABLE SOUP

Swedish

4 SERVINGS

2 lb. neck end of lamb	1 parsnip
3 pints water	$\frac{1}{2}$ celeriac
1 tablespoon salt	1 small leek
6 white peppercorns	1 small packet frozen peas
1 bay leaf	2 tablespoons flour
2 oz. butter	chopped parsley
1 carrot	

Put water and spices in soup pot and bring to the boil. Cut meat into convenient pieces and brown in butter. Pick out meat and place in boiling water, leaving butter in frying pan. Allow meat to simmer for about 2 hours. In the meantime, clean root vegetables and cut into $\frac{1}{2}$-inch cubes or slice. Brown them in remaining butter. Sprinkle flour on top and brown too, stirring when necessary. Take cup of soup and add to vegetables, cover and simmer in frying pan for 30 minutes. De-frost peas and chop parsley. When meat is tender, remove from soup, take out bones, cut into smaller pieces. Skim off excess fat from soup, add meat and vegetables with their stock, peas and parsley. Bring to the boil, season to taste and serve.

BROWN BEAN SOUP

Danish

6 SERVINGS

1 lb. dried brown beans   1 tablespoon flour
2 lb. piece of bacon   4 pints water
1 bay leaf   salt
2 oz. butter

Soak bacon overnight in cold water which is then discarded.
Soak beans separately overnight in 2 pints water. Bring
beans to the boil in same water, add bay leaf and simmer
until soft, 2—3 hours. At the same time put bacon to boil in
separate saucepan with 2 pints water. Simmer until beans
are ready. Skim off fat from bacon stock and put piece of
bacon aside. Melt butter in large saucepan and stir in flour.
Add bacon stock gradually whilst stirring. Season to taste.
Then add beans in their stock. Bring to the boil and serve
with sliced bacon.

CREAM OF MUSHROOM SOUP

Swedish

4 SERVINGS

12 oz. mushrooms $\frac{1}{2}$ teaspoon Worcestershire sauce
2 oz. butter   1 tin consommé (10$\frac{1}{2}$ oz.)
2 tablespoons chopped   or $\frac{1}{2}$ pint beef stock
  onions   1 pint milk
2 tablespoons flour   3 tablespoons double cream
1 teaspoon salt   pepper

Clean mushrooms and chop finely. Melt butter in large
saucepan and sauté mushrooms and onions for 5 minutes.

Sprinkle with flour and stir until well blended. Gradually add consommé and seasoning, stirring until smooth. Add milk and cream and simmer for 10 minutes. It is now ready to serve.

WINTER PEA SOUP

Danish

6 SERVINGS

1 lb. yellow split peas	1 celeriac
2 lb. lightly salted pork	1 teaspoon thyme
2 leeks	5 pints water

Soak peas overnight in cold water. Put to boil in 3 pints water. Cover and simmer until tender, which can take up to 3 hours. In meantime, put pork to boil separately in 2 pints water, thyme, diced celeriac and cut up leeks. Simmer until pork is tender, about 1½ hours. Arrange it so that pork and peas are ready together. Force peas through fine sieve and add stock from pork. Place vegetables in bottom of soup terrine and pour in soup. Serve pork sliced on separate serving dish. This soup is a complete meal in itself and is served with boiled potatoes. It is served on soup plates and pork and potatoes are added to each plate when at the table.

SPINACH SOUP

Swedish

4 SERVINGS

1½ pints beef stock
4 oz. spinach
1 oz. butter
1 egg yolk

1 carton double cream
(2·7 fluid oz.)
chopped parsley
salt and pepper

Wash spinach carefully, chop and drain. Melt butter in saucepan, add spinach, cover and cook gently for about 5 minutes, or until spinach turns dark. Heat stock. Stir egg yolk and cream in soup tureen until well mixed. Pour in hot bouillon while stirring. Add spinach and parsley. Season to taste and serve immediately.

FRESH PEA SOUP

Swedish

6 SERVINGS

2 lb. fresh peas in pods
2 pints water
1 bay leaf
1 teaspoon salt

2 oz. butter
4 tablespoons flour
1 pint chicken broth
½ pint single cream

Wash pods, drain and take out peas. Put pods in large saucepan with water, salt and bay leaf. Bring to the boil, cover and simmer for 45 minutes. Strain and put liquid back in pan. Add peas, bring to the boil and simmer for 10 minutes. Pass through fine sieve. Melt butter in pan and stir in flour. Add purée of peas, chicken broth and cream. Simmer until smooth and season to taste. Serve with croûtons.

Sauces play an important part in Scandinavian cooking, and it is here that the French influence is most noticeable. Many of the sauces require mushrooms, and different varieties can be used. I have, however, only mentioned the cultivated kind in the recipes as they are the most readily available here. But in Scandinavia almost every family takes trips to the country in the autumn for the express purpose of gathering wild mushrooms. It is quite difficult to be able to distinguish the edible from the poisonous kinds and many housewives in Scandinavia take pride in the number of varieties they know. On the whole, their preparation is the same, so if you like you may substitute chanterelles for the usual cultivated sort.

Sweet sauces will be found at the end of this section.

CHEESE SAUCE

Swedish

4 SERVINGS

3 oz. grated Parmesan chesse   ¾ pint milk
2 oz. butter   salt and pepper
2 tablespoons flour

Melt 1 oz. butter in saucepan and stir in flour. Add milk gradually, stirring vigorously. Season to taste with salt and pepper. Simmer for 10 minutes. Remove from heat and add rest of butter. Then carefully stir in grated cheese, using a fork. Serve immediately with fish or vegetables.

SAUCE FOR FISH OR VEGETABLES

Swedish

4 SERVINGS

¼ pint fish or vegetable   6 tablespoons double
    stock   cream
3 oz. butter   lemon juice
1 tablespoon flour   salt and pepper
3 egg yolks

Melt half the butter in a small cast iron pot. Remove from heat. Stir in flour, egg yolks and cream. Place the pot in a saucepan with hot water and let it heat, beating constantly. When sauce starts to thicken, stock should be added gradually while continuing to beat. Season to taste with salt, pepper and drops of lemon juice. Stir in rest of the butter. Sauce should be smooth and thick. Serve immediately, but if it must be kept a while, let it stand in the water bath and stir it from time to time. This sauce can be flavoured with chopped onion, parsley, capers, tomato purée, anchovy paste or shrimps.

FINE FISH SAUCE

Swedish

4 SERVINGS

3 egg yolks
¼ teaspoon freshly ground pepper
2 tablespoons vinegar
cayenne pepper

4 tablespoons cold water
5½ oz. butter
lemon juice

Put pepper, water and vinegar in a small cast iron pot and simmer until reduced to about 2 tablespoons. Remove from heat and strain out as much of the pepper as possible. Rinse pot and replace liquid. Melt butter separately. Place cast iron pot in a saucepan with hot water. Beat in egg yolks. Let the sauce get hot enough to thicken, but water must not be too hot to put your finger in, as then sauce may curdle. When sauce starts to thicken, add a little melted butter. Keep adding butter gradually, beating constantly, until it is all mixed in. Season to taste with drops of lemon juice and cayenne pepper. The sauce should be smooth and thick when ready. Serve immediately, but if it must be kept for a while, let it stay in the water bath and stir from time to time. It is delicious with fine fish or vegetables.

MUSHROOM SAUCE FOR FISH DISHES

Norwegian

6 SERVINGS

1 pint fish stock	3 tablespoons flour
4 oz. mushrooms	1½ oz. butter
¼ pint dry white wine	salt and pepper
¼ pint cream	

Trim mushrooms if necessary and cut them up rather finely. Let them sauté in a little of the butter in a saucepan. Melt rest of butter in another saucepan and stir in flour. Add fish stock (made by boiling some fish scraps in water for 20 minutes and straining) a little at a time, stirring continuously so that the texture becomes smooth. Simmer for 5 minutes. Add mushrooms and cream and bring to the boil again. Then add wine and salt and pepper to taste. Simmer for a few more minutes and serve with fish.

CURRANT SAUCE

Swedish

4 SERVINGS

3 tablespoons currants	1½ tablespoons vinegar
1 oz. butter	1 tablespoon brown sugar
2 tablespoons flour	2 teaspoons cold butter
1 pint fish stock	salt and pepper

Make stock by boiling fish scraps in 1 pint water for about 20 minutes. Strain stock before using. Rinse currants carefully in lukewarm water. Melt 1 oz. butter in a saucepan. Stir in flour, add stock little by little, stirring constantly and letting sauce thicken before more stock is added. Season the sauce lightly with salt and pepper, add currants and simmer for 10 minutes. Season to taste with sugar and vinegar. Remove from flame and stir in cold butter. Serve with fish cakes.

CAPER SAUCE

Swedish

4 SERVINGS

2 tablespoons chopped capers
1 oz. butter
2 tablespoons flour
1 pint fish stock
½ teaspoon sugar

2 teaspoons vinegar (from capers)
1 egg yolk
1 tablespoon cream
1 teaspoon butter
salt and pepper

Melt butter in saucepan and stir in flour. Heat fish stock (made by boiling fish scraps in lightly salted water then straining) and add very gradually, stirring continuously. Let sauce thicken each time before more stock is added. Stir in sugar, chopped capers and vinegar. Season to taste. The sauce should have a strong sweet and sour flavour, and a little extra vinegar can be added if so desired. Mix together egg yolk and cream and add to the sauce whilst stirring vigorously. Add teaspoon cold butter and sauce is ready to be served with boiled fish.

A good variation on this sauce for those who do not like the sweet and sour flavour is obtained by omitting the sugar and 1 teaspoon vinegar.

STRONG FISH SAUCE

Swedish

4 SERVINGS

1 hard-boiled egg yolk
1 raw egg yolk
½ teaspoon French mustard
1 teaspoon sugar

¼ teaspoon salt
1 tablespoon vinegar
¼ pint double cream
pepper

Place cold, hard-boiled egg yolk in a bowl and mash it well. Mix in raw egg yolk, making sure there are no lumps. Stir in all the seasonings. Beat cream until fairly thick and add to the bowl, stirring in with a few strokes only. Taste and season again if necessary. Serve immediately with either hot or cold fish.

If the sauce should curdle, mix in some more unbeaten cream and it will become smooth again.

SHRIMP SAUCE

Swedish

4 SERVINGS

4—6 oz. peeled shrimps
1 oz. butter
2 tablespoons flour
¾ pint fish stock

1 small tin evaporated milk
(equivalent to ¾ pt. diluted)
1 teaspoon cold butter
salt and pepper

Melt butter in a saucepan and stir in flour to a smooth paste. Add hot fish stock gradually, stirring constantly. When it has thickened, stir in evaporated milk and simmer for 5 minutes. Add shrimps and season to taste. Leave on the flame long enough to heat shrimps thoroughly, but do not let them boil. Remove from heat and add cold butter. Serve with any boiled or baked fish.

This sauce can be made with tinned mussels instead of shrimps, but take care that the mussels are in their natural brine.

SWEDISH MAYONNAISE

4—8 SERVINGS

2 egg yolks
1 tablespoon vinegar
½ teaspoon salt
1 teaspoon French mustard

¾ pint oil
pinch cayenne pepper
2 tablespoons boiling
   water

All ingredients should be slightly warm.

Place a round-bottomed bowl on a cloth wrung out in cold water. Mix egg yolks, vinegar and spices thoroughly, using a good egg whisk. Add the oil, a few drops at a time, beating continuously, until it is all mixed in. The mayonnaise should then be very thick and smooth. Stir in 2 tablespoons boiling water, which gives it a nice consistency and makes it keep longer.

MILD SALAD SAUCE

Swedish

4 SERVINGS

2 egg yolks
2 tablespoons water
2½ tablespoons oil
1 tablespoon lemon juice

¼ teaspoon salt
6 tablespoons double cream
¼ teaspoon sugar

Put all ingredients except cream in a bowl and mix well. Place bowl over a saucepan of hot water. Heat water sufficiently for sauce to thicken, beating constantly, but do not let it boil. When sauce is thick and smooth, remove from water bath. Beat from time to time until cool. Beat cream separately and carefully mix into the sauce.

This sauce is used for salads in the same way as mayonnaise, and can be flavoured with mustard, tomato paste, chili sauce, etc.

FINE STEAK SAUCE

Swedish

4 SERVINGS

3 egg yolks
¼ teaspoon freshly ground pepper
1 tablespoon chopped onion
2 tablespoons vinegar

4 tablespoons cold water
5½ oz. butter
2 tablespoons chopped parsley
cayenne pepper and salt

Place chopped onions, pepper, vinegar and water in a small cast iron pot and simmer until the liquid is reduced to about 2 tablespoons. Remove from heat and strain out the onion and as much of the pepper as possible. Rinse pot and replace liquid. Stir in egg yolks and 1 oz. butter. Place pot over saucepan of hot water. Beat constantly whilst water heats, but do not let it get too hot as sauce will then curdle. When sauce begins to thicken the butter should be added a little at a time, while continuing to beat. Add parsley and season to taste with cayenne pepper and salt. The sauce should be thick and smooth. It is best to serve sauce immediately, but if it must be kept a while, let it stand in water bath and stir from time to time. This sauce is delicious with steak, roast beef or veal fillet.

TOMATO AND MUSHROOM SAUCE

Swedish

4 SERVINGS

3 tinned tomatoes
5 oz. mushrooms
2½ oz. butter
¼ pint meat stock
3 tablespoons chopped onions

6 tablespoons dry white wine
1½ tablespoons chopped parsley
½ tablespoon potato flour
salt and pepper

Clean and slice mushrooms. Melt 2 oz. butter in frying pan and add mushrooms. Season with salt and pepper and fry slowly for 20 minutes. Cut up tomatoes, remove seeds and add to pan together with onions, wine and stock. Simmer for 5 minutes and add parsley. Mix flour in a little cold stock and stir into sauce. Bring to the boil whilst stirring. Remove from heat, season to taste and add rest of butter. Serve with pork or veal.

MUSHROOM SAUCE

Swedish

4 SERVINGS

4 oz. mushrooms
2 oz. butter
2 tablespoons flour

1 pint milk or 1 pint chicken
bouillon and cream
1 tablespoon sherry
salt and pepper

Slice mushrooms and place in saucepan with butter. Sauté covered for 5 minutes. Season to taste with salt and pepper. Stir in flour and add liquid gradually, stirring constantly, until sauce is smooth and thick. Simmer for a few minutes, add sherry and season to taste. Serve with meat dishes.

TOMATO SAUCE

Swedish

4 SERVINGS

3 tablespoons tomato purée
$\frac{3}{4}$ pint meat stock
4 tablespoons Madeira wine
sugar if desired

$\frac{1}{2}$ tablespoon potato flour
$\frac{1}{2}$ oz. butter
salt and pepper

Put wine in saucepan and simmer until reduced by half. Stir in tomato purée and stock and let it come to the boil. Mix flour in little cold stock and add to sauce while beating vigorously. Bring to the boil again, remove from heat, season to taste (with sugar if desired) and stir in butter. Serve with pork.

RED WINE SAUCE

Swedish

4 SERVINGS

¼ pint meat stock
1 tablespoon sugar
¾ pint red wine
2½ oz. pearl onions
3½ oz. mixed vegetables
   (carrots, parsnip, leek, celery)

3½ oz. lean ham
2 oz. butter
2½ tablespoons flour
water
salt

Peel onions and boil for 3 minutes in a little salted water. Drain well and discard water. Place onions in saucepan with ¼ pint wine and sugar and simmer on low flame for 30 minutes, or until soft. Dice ham and vegetables quite finely. Fry in butter until nicely browned. Stir in flour and let it brown as well. Whilst stirring, gradually add rest of wine and stock. Let sauce simmer for 10 minutes. Strain it and add to the onions in their sauce. Stir until smooth and season if necessary. Serve with boiled ham or pork roast.

SAVOURY SAUCE

Swedish

4 SERVINGS

2 tablespoons meat dripping
2 tablespoons flour
¾ pint meat stock
2 tablespoons chopped onions
5 tablespoons vinegar

1 oz. butter
1 tablespoon chopped parsley
1 pickled gherkin (thinly
    sliced)
salt and pepper

Make a basic sauce by melting dripping, stirring in flour
and gradually adding stock, stirring continuously. Simmer
for 10 minutes. Fry onions slowly in butter until starting
to brown. Add vinegar and simmer until liquid is reduced
by half. Add this to basic sauce and simmer for another
10 minutes. Remove from heat and add parsley and gherkins.
Season to taste with salt and pepper. Serve with pork or veal.

FINE SAUCE FOR PORK

Swedish

4—6 SERVINGS

2 tablespoons pork dripping
2 tablespoons flour
¾ pint meat stock
3 oz. mushrooms
2 tablespoons oil
3 oz. lean ham

2 tablespoons chopped onions
¼ pint dry white wine
2 tablespoons tomato purée
1 tablespoon chopped parsley
salt and pepper

Make a basic sauce by melting dripping in frying pan,
stirring in flour and gradually adding stock while continuing
to stir. Simmer for 10 minutes. Clean mushrooms, slice
and fry in oil slowly until slightly browned. This will take

up to 20 minutes. Then add chopped onion and ham and fry for another 2 minutes. Add wine and simmer until liquid is reduced by half. Add this to basic sauce, together with tomato purée and parsley. Season with salt and pepper to taste and simmer for another 5 minutes. Serve with pork roast or fillet.

ONION SAUCE (1)

Swedish

4 SERVINGS

3 medium chopped onions
2 tablespoons pork dripping
2 tablespoons flour
¾ pint meat stock

1½ oz. butter
¼ pint dry white wine
salt and pepper

Make the basic sauce by melting dripping in a frying pan, stirring in flour and adding stock gradually whilst stirring. Simmer for 10 minutes. Melt butter and slowly fry onions until starting to brown. Add wine and simmer until liquid is reduced by half. Add this to basic sauce, season to taste with salt and pepper and simmer for another 10 minutes. Serve with meat and vegetables.

ONION SAUCE (2)

Swedish

4 SERVINGS

3 chopped onions	1 pint milk
1 oz. butter	1¼ teaspoons salt
2 tablespoons flour	pepper

Melt butter in saucepan, add onions and sauté until soft and transparent. Stir in flour. Add milk gradually, stirring until smooth and sauce has thickened. Simmer for a few minutes, season to taste and serve with fried pork.

LEMON SAUCE

Swedish

4 SERVINGS

juice of ½ lemon	1 small tin evaporated milk
1 oz. butter	(equivalent to ¾ pint diluted)
2 tablespoons flour	1 egg yolk
¾ pint fish stock	2 tablespoons top of the milk
1 teaspoon cold butter	salt and pepper

Melt butter in saucepan and stir in flour to a smooth paste. Add fish stock gradually, stirring constantly. When it has thickened, stir in evaporated milk and simmer for 5 minutes. Season with lemon juice, salt and pepper. Mix egg yolk and milk together and stir into sauce. Remove from the heat and add cold butter. Serve with any boiled or baked fish.

FRICASSÉE SAUCE WITH CURRY

Swedish

4 SERVINGS

2 teaspoons curry powder
1½ oz. butter
2 tablespoons flour

¾ pint stock
1 egg yolk
2 teaspoons cream

Melt 1 oz. butter in saucepan and stir in flour. Add stock gradually (using the appropriate kind) whilst stirring vigorously until sauce is smooth and thick. Simmer for 10 minutes. Mix curry powder, yolk and cream and add to sauce whilst stirring. Bring to boil again, remove from heat and stir in rest of butter. Serve with fricassée chicken or veal.

PAPRIKA SAUCE

Swedish

4 SERVINGS

2 teaspoons paprika
2 oz. butter
2 tablespoons flour
¾ pint chicken stock

2 tablespoons chopped onion
¼ pint white wine
salt and pepper

Melt 1 oz. butter in saucepan and stir in flour. Add stock gradually whilst stirring vigorously. Simmer for 10 minutes, stirring from time to time. Fry onion slowly in rest of butter until transparent. Add wine and simmer until liquid is reduced by half. Add this to basic sauce and stir in paprika. Season to taste with salt and pepper and simmer for another 10 minutes. The sauce should be rose-coloured and highly seasoned. Serve with boiled chicken or veal.

CREAM SAUCE FOR FOWL

Swedish

4 SERVINGS

2 tablespoons fowl dripping
2 tablespoons flour
½ pint stock
1 teaspoon butter

¼ pint double cream
1 teaspoon currant jelly
salt and pepper

Melt the dripping and stir in flour, letting it brown a little. Gradually add stock, stirring continuously. Add cream and simmer for 10 minutes, stirring from time to time. Season to taste with salt, pepper and currant jelly. Add butter and serve. This sauce goes well with any roast fowl.

VANILLA SAUCE

Swedish

4 SERVINGS

½ pint milk
1 vanilla pod
3 egg yolks

2 tablespoons sugar
2 tablespoons double cream

Pour milk into a small cast iron pot. Cut vanilla pod into small pieces and add to the milk. Bring to the boil, remove from heat, cover and stand for 5 minutes. Beat egg yolks and sugar until white and fluffy. Strain milk to remove vanilla pod and stir into egg mixture. Pour contents back into pot and simmer on very low flame, beating vigorously all the time, until sauce has thickened. (It is important not to let sauce boil, to prevent curdling.) Let it cool completely, stirring from time to time. Beat cream until thick, add vanilla sauce and stir in gently. Chill, and serve with fruit pie or apple cake.

LIQUEUR SAUCE

Swedish

4 SERVINGS

½ pint water
4 tablespoons sugar
1 teaspoon potato flour

¼ pint liqueur
red or green colouring

Mix water, sugar and flour and bring to the boil, stirring constantly. Add liqueur and colouring (according to which liqueur is used). The flavour should be strong. Serve warm with ice cream or pancakes.

CARAMEL SAUCE (1)

Swedish

4 SERVINGS

6 oz. sugar ¼ pint water

Put sugar in clean, lukewarm frying pan. Let it melt on fairly low flame, stirring with wooden spoon. When melted and a golden colour, it is ready. Take care it does not turn too dark, as that will give a burnt flavour. Add boiling water and let the sauce continue to simmer, stirring constantly until smooth. Pour into sauce bowl and serve hot or cold with junket or ice cream.

CARAMEL SAUCE (2)

3 tablespoons sugar
1 teaspoon cocoa

¼ pint double cream
1 teaspoon butter

Mix cocoa and sugar in small cast iron pot. Add cream and butter. Bring to the boil while stirring. Simmer until it starts to thicken. Remove from heat and stir until cool. Serve cool or lukewarm with ice cream.

SWEET SAUCE

Swedish

4 SERVINGS

5 tablespoons golden syrup
¾ pint milk or cream

2 teaspoons cocoa
1½ teaspoons potato flour

Place syrup in clean, lukewarm frying pan and simmer while stirring for 5 minutes. Stir in milk and simmer until smooth. Mix cocoa and flour together with a little cold water. Stir this into the sauce, and let it just come to the boil. Sauce is then ready to be served with a pudding.

SWEET LEMON SAUCE

Swedish

4 SERVINGS

2 egg yolks
½ pint milk
2 tablespoons sugar
½ tablespoon potato flour

1 teaspoon grated lemon peel
¼ pint double cream
1 tablespoon lemon juice

Mix egg yolks, milk, flour, sugar and grated lemon peel in a small cast iron pot. Bring to the boil while stirring vigorously. Simmer until it is thick and creamy, remove from heat and stir until cool. Stir in lemon juice and whipped cream. Serve with any cooked fruit sweet, such as apple pie, etc.

ORANGE SAUCE

Swedish

4 SERVINGS

2 egg yolks   1 orange
1 egg white   juice of $\frac{1}{2}$ lemon
6 tablespoons icing sugar $\frac{1}{4}$ pint double cream

Wash and dry orange, grate the yellow peel. Peel off the white pith and discard. Dice orange finely. Beat sugar and egg yolks well, add orange and grated peel. Stir in lemon juice. Beat egg white and cream separately until stiff. Fold into the sauce. Serve with any cooked fruit sweet.

WINE SAUCE

Swedish

4 SERVINGS

3 egg yolks   3 tablespoons water
$1\frac{1}{2}$ tablespoons sugar   1 teaspoon grated lemon peel
$\frac{1}{4}$ pint white wine   2 teaspoons lemon juice

Put all ingredients except lemon juice in small cast iron pot. Bring to the boil while stirring vigorously. Simmer until thick and foamy. Add lemon juice and serve hot with pancakes or stewed fruit.

A good variation on this sauce is to stir in 3 tablespoons whipped cream before serving.

CHOCOLATE SAUCE

Swedish

4 SERVINGS

3½ tablespoons cocoa   ½ pint water
3 tablespoons sugar   1 teaspoon vanilla essence
½ tablespoon potato flour   ¼ pint double cream

Mix cocoa, sugar and flour in saucepan. Add water and bring to the boil while stirring vigorously. Remove from heat and stir in whipped cream, seasoned with vanilla essence. Serve either warm or cold with ice cream.

DARK CHOCOLATE SAUCE

Swedish

4 SERVINGS

5 oz. block chocolate   ¼ pint water

Chop chocolate and place in double saucepan. Heat until chocolate is entirely melted. Add boiling water while stirring. Bring sauce to the boil and let it simmer until thick and smooth. Serve immediately with ice cream.

LUNCHEON DISHES

Many people have their main meal in the evening and prefer an easily prepared, light luncheon. A tasty casserole or omelette can therefore be just the right dish. Omelettes in particular are very popular in Scandinavia and are served with a variety of interesting fillings.

The Mixed Pan is also recommended. It is very easy to make as well as being economical, as it is usually prepared from leftover meat and potatoes.

HOT MINCED MEAT SANDWICH

Swedish

4 SERVINGS

10 oz. minced beef
3 tablespoons breadcrumbs
¼ pint milk
2 tablespoons chopped onions
1 tablespoon chopped capers

2 tablespoons chopped,
  pickled beetroot
2½ oz. butter
4 large slices white bread
salt and pepper

Place breadcrumbs and milk in a bowl and mix in meat until smooth. Add chopped onions, beetroot and capers, mixing well. Season to taste with salt and pepper. Brown about a third of butter and fry bread slices on one side. Take them out and spread a quarter of the mince on fried side of each slice. Brown another third of butter and place sandwiches with meat side down in frying pan. Fry until evenly brown. Add rest of butter and fry other side of bread. Place on heated dish and serve immediately.

MEAT CAKES WITH BACON AND CHEESE

Swedish

6 SERVINGS

1 lb. minced beef
4 oz. minced veal
1 egg
6 tablespoons breadcrumbs
½ pint milk

6 slices back bacon
6 slices cheese
1 oz. butter
salt and pepper

Mix egg, milk and breadcrumbs. Add minced meat and stir well until smooth and creamy. Season to taste with salt and pepper. Form into 6 cakes and wind a slice of bacon around each one, securing it with a toothpick. Melt butter in an oven pan and place meat cakes in it. Bake in heated oven (Regulo 8—475° F.) for 20—25 minutes, basting with fat from time to time. After 15 minutes, place a thick slice of cheese over each one and replace in oven. Serve when cheese is mostly melted, with green salad.

BACON CASSEROLE

Swedish

4 SERVINGS

1 lb. leeks	4 tablespoons grated cheese
1½ oz. butter	1 egg yolk
2 tablespoons flour	8 rashers bacon
¾ pint milk	salt and pepper

Clean leeks well and slice. Place in saucepan with 1 oz. butter, cover and simmer until soft. Season lightly and place in a shallow, buttered oven dish. Melt rest of butter in same saucepan, stir in flour and gradually add milk while continuing to stir, until sauce is thick and smooth. Season lightly with salt and pepper. Remove from heat and stir in 3 tablespoons cheese and egg yolk. Pour sauce over leeks so that they are completely covered. Sprinkle rest of cheese on top. Cut bacon across grain to make short strips. Place these over top so that it is completely covered. Bake in heated oven (Regulo 9—500° F.) or put under grill until bacon is crisp. Serve with boiled or fried potatoes.

HAM CASSEROLE

Danish

4 SERVINGS

6½ oz. smoked ham
3 tablespoons grated cheese
6½ oz. macaroni
3 eggs

½ pint milk
salt and pepper
½ oz. butter

Boil macaroni in salted water until barely soft. Rinse in plenty of cold water and drain well. Dice ham and fry lightly in butter. Mix macaroni, ham and cheese in bowl. Beat eggs and milk, seasoned with salt and pepper. Stir into macaroni mixture, seasoning to taste. Pour into buttered casserole and bake in heated oven (Regulo 5—400° F.) for about 40 minutes. Serve with mushroom or tomato sauce.

TOMATO AND LEEK CASSEROLE

Swedish

4 SERVINGS

6 tomatoes
6 leeks
2 oz. butter
2 eggs

2 teaspoons flour
½ pint milk
salt and pepper

Wash and dry tomatoes, clean and slice leeks. Melt 1 oz. butter in frying pan, add leeks and let them fry slowly until tender. Season lightly with salt and pepper. Slice tomatoes and fry in same manner, keeping leeks hot. Butter casserole and place tomatoes and leeks in it. Beat eggs, flour and milk. Season lightly and pour into casserole. Place in heated oven (Regulo 7—450° F.) for about 30 minutes, when it should be golden colour. Serve with fried potatoes.

ONION CASSEROLE

Swedish

4 SERVINGS

4 medium onions
10 oz. minced veal and pork
2 oz. margarine
4 tablespoons breadcrumbs

6 tablespoons cream
6 tablespoons water
¼ pint stock
salt and pepper

Peel and slice onions. Melt margarine in frying pan, add onion and let it fry slowly until golden brown. Place breadcrumbs in a bowl and add water and cream. Stir in minced meat, mixing very well. Season to taste with salt and pepper. Place half the fried onions in a casserole so that they cover the bottom. Place mince in a layer on top and spread rest of onions over it. Pour stock over, making some holes with a fork so that it seeps through. Bake in heated oven (Regulo 5—400° F.) for about 45 minutes. If onions are getting too brown, place a cover over the casserole. Serve with boiled or mashed potatoes.

FRANKFURTER AND MUSHROOM CASSEROLE

Swedish

4 SERVINGS

4 frankfurters
4 tomatoes
2 tablespoons grated cheese

½ oz. butter
stewed mushrooms
(see page 102)

Prepare stewed mushrooms as directed on page 102. Butter a casserole. Slice frankfurters and spread over bottom of casserole. Pour stewed mushrooms over. Slice tomatoes and spread over mushrooms. Sprinkle cheese on top and dot with butter. Bake in heated oven (Regulo 7—450° F.) for 20 minutes. Serve with fried potatoes.

MIXED PAN

Swedish

4 SERVINGS

12 oz. leftover meat
12 oz. cold boiled potatoes
2 onions

2 oz. margarine
salt and pepper

Use any leftover meat and dice it finely. Dice potatoes in same way. Chop onions. Melt some of the margarine and fry onions golden. Keep them warm in a dish. Add rest of margarine to frying pan and fry potatoes until they are turning brown. Add meat and let it fry also, mixing it well with potatoes. Mix in fried onions and season to taste with salt and pepper. Serve with fried eggs.

MIXED VEGETABLE POT

Swedish

4 SERVINGS

1 large cauliflower
8 small onions
4 tomatoes
2½ oz. margarine

¼ pint cream
2 tablespoons chopped
  parsley
salt and pepper

Clean cauliflower and divide into pieces. Peel onions and quarter tomatoes. Melt margarine in cast iron pot and mix in cream. Arrange vegetables in pot and season with salt and pepper. Sprinkle parsley over, cover and simmer for 30 minutes. If cream evaporates too much add a little more, as the dish should be moist. Serve directly from pot with fried potatoes.

TOMATOES STUFFED WITH MUSHROOMS

Swedish

4 SERVINGS

8 medium tomatoes	6 rashers bacon
8 oz. mushrooms	2 tablespoons grated cheese
2 oz. butter	1 tablespoon breadcrumbs
2 tablespoons flour	salt and pepper
¼ pint cream	

Wash and dry tomatoes. Slice off top of each one and remove pulp. Season inside with a little salt and pepper. Clean and chop mushrooms. Fry them in 1½ oz. butter. Season with salt and pepper and when browned a little sprinkle in flour. Stir well and add cream and tomato pulp. Simmer for 5 minutes then cool before filling tomatoes. Replace tops and put tomatoes close together in shallow buttered oven dish. Chop bacon and sprinkle over tomatoes together with cheese and breadcrumbs. Dot with rest of butter and bake in heated oven (Regulo 7—450° F.) for 20 minutes. Serve immediately.

SPINACH RING WITH HAM

Swedish

4—6 SERVINGS

1 lb. frozen chopped spinach	1¾ pints milk
4 eggs	6½ oz. smoked ham
3 tablespoons flour	salt and pepper

De-frost and drain spinach. Beat eggs with 1 tablespoon flour and add ¾ pint milk. Season with salt and pepper. Add spinach and stir well. Butter a ring-shaped form and pour in spinach mixture. Cook in bain marie for 30 minutes. Dice ham and fry. (If very lean, some butter may be required.) Stir in 2 tablespoons flour and gradually add 1 pint milk while continuing to stir. Simmer for 5 minutes and season if necessary. When spinach is set, turn it out on a warm dish and pour ham sauce in the centre.

SPINACH PUDDING

Danish

4 SERVINGS

1 lb. chopped frozen spinach	salt
2 eggs	butter
3 tablespoons cream	4 slices toast

De-frost spinach and pour off water. Beat eggs and cream and mix well with spinach. Season to taste with salt. Butter 4 small forms and divide spinach between them. Place in bain marie and boil for 20 minutes, when they should be stiff. Make toast, butter the slices and turn out a pudding on each one. Serve immediately.

BAKED SPINACH WITH CHEESE

Danish

4 SERVINGS

1 lb. chopped frozen spinach
3 tablespoons cream
2 oz. butter

5 tablespoons grated
   cheese
salt

De-frost spinach and drain off water. Melt 1 oz. butter in saucepan and stir in spinach, cream and 4 tablespoons grated cheese. Season to taste with salt. Butter a casserole and pour in spinach. Sprinkle rest of cheese on top and dot with 1 oz. butter. Bake in heated oven (Regulo 5—400° F.) for about 30 minutes or until cheese is melted. Serve with eggs.

CAULIFLOWER, TOMATOES AND EGGS

Swedish

4—6 SERVINGS

2 small cauliflowers
4 tomatoes
3 eggs
¾ pint milk

1 tablespoon flour
3 tablespoons grated cheese
salt and pepper

Clean cauliflowers and remove coarse leaves and stalk. Boil in salted water until nearly soft. Place them whole in a large buttered casserole. Slice tomatoes and place in a ring around cauliflowers. Beat eggs, flour and milk and season with salt and pepper. Pour this over the cauliflowers and sprinkle cheese on top. Bake in heated oven (Regulo 7—450° F.) for about 30 minutes. Serve with fried potatoes or sausages.

EGG AND ONION CASSEROLE

Swedish

4 SERVINGS

6 hard-boiled eggs
2 large onions
2½ oz. butter
3 tablespoons flour

¾ pint milk
2 tablespoons grated cheese
salt and pepper

Peel, slice and fry onions in 1 oz. butter. Place in a casserole so that the bottom is covered. Peel and slice eggs and spread over onions. Melt rest of butter in saucepan and stir in flour. Gradually add milk, while continuing to stir. Let sauce simmer for 10 minutes. Stir in grated cheese and season to taste with salt and pepper. Pour sauce into casserole and place high in heated oven (Regulo 9—500° F.) or under grill until slightly browned on top. Serve with fried potatoes.

EGGS IN CHEESE SAUCE
WITH FRANKFURTERS

Swedish

4 SERVINGS

8 frankfurters
6 hard-boiled eggs
3 oz. margarine
3 tablespoons flour
¾ pint milk

4 oz. processed cheese
1 tablespoon chopped parsley
4 slices white bread
½ teaspoon salt
pepper

Shell hard-boiled eggs and quarter them. Melt margarine in saucepan and stir in flour. Gradually add milk, stirring constantly until sauce is smooth. Cut up cheese and add together with salt and pepper. Cover and simmer on low heat for about 15 minutes or until cheese is melted. Stir and add eggs, bring to boiling point and keep warm. Split frankfurters, cut in half and put under grill to get crisp and brown. Toast bread and cut into triangles. Pour creamed eggs on to hot serving dish and sprinkle with parsley. Place toast and frankfurters alternately around and serve.

EGG CASSEROLE

Swedish

4 SERVINGS

4 frankfurters	3 eggs
1 tablespoon tomato purée	1 tablespoon flour
2 tablespoons grated cheese	¾ pint milk
2 oz. butter	salt and pepper

Melt butter in casserole. Cut frankfurters in halves and split lengthwise. Spread some tomato purée on flat side of each frankfurter. Place them in casserole round side down, sprinkle with cheese. Beat eggs in a bowl together with flour. Beat in milk and season with salt and pepper. Pour batter into casserole and bake in heated oven (Regulo 7—450° F.) for 20—30 minutes. Serve with fried potatoes.

OMELETTE

Swedish

4 SERVINGS

4 eggs
1 pint milk
4 teaspoons flour

2 oz. butter
salt

Mix ½ pint milk with flour. Add rest of milk while beating and then the eggs one at a time. Melt butter in shallow casserole. Pour in batter and bake in heated oven (Regulo 7—450° F.) for about 20 minutes, or until slightly brown. Serve with stewed mushrooms, fish or spinach.

COUNTRY OMELETTE

Swedish

6 SERVINGS

4 boiled potatoes
4 frankfurters
2 tablespoons chopped chives
2 tomatoes

6 eggs
4 tablespoons cream
2 oz. butter
salt and pepper

Slice potatoes and fry golden brown on both sides in some of the butter. Put aside and keep warm. Slice frankfurters and fry in rest of butter. Mix in fried potatoes and sliced tomatoes. Sprinkle with chopped chives and seasoning. Beat eggs and cream and pour into pan. Make some holes with fork, cover, and fry slowly, shaking pan from time to time to prevent burning. Serve when completely set.

FILLED PANCAKES

Swedish

4—6 SERVINGS

3 eggs
5½ oz. self-raising flour
1½ pints milk
2 oz. butter
½ teaspoon salt
butter for frying

Filling:
8 oz. mushrooms
4 oz. shrimps
2 tablespoons chopped onion
3 oz. butter
2 tablespoons flour
1 small tin evaporated milk
(equivalent to ¾ pint diluted)
1 tablespoon dry sherry
salt and pepper
water
grated cheese
butter

Beat eggs in large bowl. Add flour and salt whilst stirring then add milk gradually. Beat until well blended. Melt butter and stir in. Stand batter for 1 hour. Melt a little butter in frying pan, pour in enough batter to cover pan and fry golden brown on both sides. Repeat until all batter is used up.

Filling: Melt butter in saucepan, add chopped mushrooms and onions and sauté until starting to colour. Season with salt and pepper. Sprinkle flour over and stir in. Dilute evaporated milk with water to make ½ pint in all, which is gradually added whilst stirring. Add shrimps and sherry. Season to taste. Divide mixture between pancakes, placing it in middle and rolling each one up. Place side by side in buttered oven dish, sprinkle with grated cheese and dot with butter. They can now stand until 15 minutes before required, when they are heated in hot oven until cheese melts. Filling can be varied according to taste.

CREAMED SWEETBREADS

Swedish

4 SERVINGS

2 pairs sweetbreads
2 pints boiling water
1 tablespoon salt
1 tablespoon lemon juice
2 oz. butter
2 tablespoons chopped onions

8 oz. sliced mushrooms
2 tablespoons flour
½ pint stock
1 tablespoon sherry
¼ pint cream
pepper

Soak sweetbreads in cold water for 1 hour. Drain, place in saucepan, pour boiling water over them. Add salt and lemon juice, bring to the boil and simmer for 20 minutes. Remove sweetbreads and cool stock quickly by immersing in cold water. Remove membranes and dice sweetbreads. If sweetbreads cannot be prepared at once, keep in cool stock. Melt butter in saucepan and stir in flour. Add stock and cream gradually, stirring until smooth and creamy. Simmer 5 minutes. Season with salt, pepper and lemon juice. Add sweetbreads and bring to the boil. Add sherry just before serving in omelette or pastry shell.

VEGETABLES

The long Scandinavian winters used to restrict the supply of fresh vegetables to the summer months. As a result, root vegetables, available all the year round, have always been very popular there. Potatoes in particular are eaten in great quantities, and are served with almost every cooked meal. The combination of a stewed vegetable and boiled potatoes is a typically Scandinavian practice. It is plain fare, but well worth trying for those who do not shy from eating a substantial meal. The ordinary ways of cooking vegetables are common to most countries, and are not included here. Minor variations can sometimes bring astonishing results, and I hope you will enjoy trying a few which have been suggested in these recipes.

STEWED MUSHROOMS

Swedish

4 SERVINGS

7 oz. mushrooms
1 teaspoon salt
2 oz. butter
2 tablespoons flour

¼ pint stock (meat,
fish or vegetable)
6 tablespoons cream
pepper

Clean mushrooms by scraping, but avoid washing unless necessary. Slice them if large. Melt butter in a cast iron pot and add mushrooms. Let them fry for about 15 minutes, season with salt and pepper. Sprinkle flour over mushrooms while stirring. Gradually add the appropriate stock and cream and simmer for 10 minutes. Serve with omelette, fish or meat.

CREAMED MUSHROOMS

Swedish

4 SERVINGS

7 oz. mushrooms
½ teaspoon salt
pepper

2 oz. butter
½ pint cream

Clean mushrooms by scraping, but avoid washing unless necessary. If large, slice them. Melt butter in small cast iron pot, add mushrooms and seasoning. Simmer for 15 minutes. Add cream and let it continue to simmer until sauce thickens, which will take up to 1 hour. Serve in omelette or with meat.

FRIED POTATOES

Swedish

4—6 SERVINGS

8 medium size boiled potatoes
1 large onion
salt and pepper

meat dripping or margarine
for frying
chopped parsley

Dice potatoes and slice onion. Fry onion golden brown in some fat. Remove and keep warm. Fry potatoes until nicely brown in just enough fat to prevent burning. It is usually quicker not to cook too much in pan at one time. When potatoes are all nicely brown mix with onions in frying pan until piping hot. Season to taste. Place in warm dish, sprinkle with chopped parsley and serve.

CREAMED ASPARAGUS

Swedish

4 SERVINGS

1 tin asparagus
2 oz. butter
3 tablespoons flour

$\frac{3}{4}$ pint asparagus
liquid and cream
salt and pepper

Melt butter in saucepan and stir in flour. Add sufficient cream to asparagus liquid to make up $\frac{3}{4}$ pint. Add this gradually to saucepan, stirring until smooth and creamy. Simmer 5 minutes and season with salt and pepper. Cut up asparagus, using scissors, and add to saucepan. Bring to the boil and remove from heat immediately. Serve with plain omelette.

POTATO CAKES

Swedish

3—4 SERVINGS

2 very large potatoes	1 teaspoon salt
2 tablespoons flour	pepper
oil for frying	

Peel potatoes and grate them into a bowl. Add salt, flour and a little pepper. Beat vigorously until smooth. Heat about 1 tablespoon oil in frying pan. Put in about 3 tablespoons of potato mixture, in separate heaps, and flatten them to thin cakes with a spatula. Fry on a fairly high flame until crisp and golden brown on both sides. Keep hot on serving dish in oven until they are all done in the same manner. Serve with bacon or sausages, or by themselves with Swedish cranberries.

SOUTHERN FRIED POTATOES

Swedish

4 SERVINGS

8 medium potatoes	2 tablespoons chopped parsley
1 large onion	dripping or margarine for frying
¼ pint single cream	salt and pepper

Peel and dice potatoes. Peel and chop onion coarsely. Warm some fat and put enough potatoes in pan to cover the bottom. Fry them on all sides until brown and soft. Put them aside and keep warm. Continue in same manner until all potatoes are fried. Brown onions. Put all back in frying pan and pour in cream. Simmer until it starts to get mushy. Season to taste with salt and pepper. Pour into warm dish, sprinkle with parsley and serve.

ROAST POTATOES WITH CHEESE

Swedish

4 SERVINGS

4 very large potatoes
4 oz. margarine
1 teaspoon salt

1 teaspoon paprika
4 tablespoons grated cheese

Peel potatoes and slice them thinly, half way through. Melt margarine in shallow casserole and turn potatoes in it. Leave potatoes in casserole, sliced side up. Sprinkle with salt and paprika. Roast in heated oven (Regulo 6—425° F.) for 45 minutes, basting frequently. Pull out casserole and sprinkle potatoes with cheese. Replace in oven and continue to roast, without basting, for another 30 minutes, or until done. Serve with roast meat.

BROWN BEANS

Swedish

4—6 SERVINGS

1 lb. dried brown beans	1½ tablespoons salt
2½ pints water	4 tablespoons treacle or molasses
3 tablespoons vinegar	2 tablespoons brown sugar

Soak beans overnight in water. Bring beans and water to the boil in a large saucepan, reduce heat and simmer slowly for 1 hour. Add all other ingredients, stir and cover. Simmer until beans are tender and in a thick sauce. If sauce does not thicken, remove cover and allow to reduce. Serve with fried pork.

STEWED PARSNIPS

Swedish

4 SERVINGS

1½ lb. parsnips	3 tablespoons double cream
1 bouillon cube	1 oz. butter
½ pint water	sugar
2 egg yolks	salt and pepper

Clean, peel and dice parsnips. Dissolve the bouillon cube in water and boil parsnips in it until they are soft. Remove from fire. Stir yolks into cream and add to the bouillon. Put on a low flame, stirring continuously until sauce thickens. Do not let it boil. Stir in butter. Season with sugar, salt and pepper to taste. Serve with any meat dish.

FRIED PARSNIPS

Swedish

4 SERVINGS

1½ lb. parsnips   3 oz. margarine
4 tablespoons flour   salt and pepper

Clean parsnips and boil them in their skins until soft. Peel
and slice them. Mix flour with some salt and pepper and
turn sliced parsnips in this. Fry them in margarine until
golden brown on each side. Serve with any meat dish.

PURÉE OF CARROTS

Swedish

4 SERVINGS

1½ lb. new carrots   3 tablespoons double cream
1 bouillon cube   salt
2 oz. butter   water

Clean and grate carrots. Dissolve bouillon cube in about
½ pint water. Add grated carrots and simmer until soft.
Strain off bouillon (which can be used for something else),
and pass carrots through a sieve. Melt butter in a saucepan
and add purée. Stir in cream and season to taste. Let it
come to the boil again before serving with any meat dish.

STEWED CARROTS

Swedish

4 SERVINGS

1½ lb. new carrots	2 tablespoons chopped parsley
1 oz. butter	salt
½ tablespoon flour	water

Scrape and clean carrots. Cut into thin 2-inch strips. Boil until soft in just enough water to cover them. In another saucepan melt butter and stir in flour. Add stock from carrots gradually, stirring constantly until smooth and all the stock is added. Put carrots and chopped parsley into sauce and simmer for a few minutes. Serve with salted meat dishes.

GLAZED CARROTS

Swedish

4 SERVINGS

1½ lb. new carrots	1 tablespoon brown sugar
1 bouillon cube	2 oz. margarine
½ pint water	

Scrape and wash carrots. Dissolve bouillon cube in water and add margarine and sugar. Simmer carrots in this until soft. Remove them and reduce sauce until it is thick. Put carrots back in and coat them with the sauce by shaking over a low flame. Serve as an additional vegetable with any roast meat.

PURÉE OF SWEDE

Swedish

4—6 SERVINGS

2 lb. swede
1 lb. potatoes
1 bouillon cube

½ teaspoon ground ginger
water

Wash, peel and dice swede and potatoes. Dissolve bouillon cube in about ½ pint hot water. Place diced vegetables in saucepan and pour bouillon over. There should be just sufficient for vegetables to simmer without burning. When soft, mash into bouillon, which should be reduced if necessary to make right consistency of purée. Mix in ginger and serve. This vegetable is usually served with any salted meat.

STRING BEANS AU GRATIN

Swedish

4 SERVINGS

1 lb. string beans
4 tomatoes
4 tablespoons grated cheese

2 oz. butter
salt and pepper

Wash string beans and remove threads. Boil in slightly salted water until tender and drain well. Butter shallow oven dish. Cut tomatoes in half and place close together in centre of casserole. Arrange string beans in a ring around tomatoes and season with a little salt and pepper. Sprinkle cheese over top and bake in heated oven, (Regulo 7—450° F.) for about 10 minutes, or until cheese is melted. Serve immediately.

GRILLED TOMATOES

Swedish

4 SERVINGS

4 large tomatoes
1 clove garlic
1 oz. soft butter

1 tablespoon chopped
parsley
salt and pepper

Cut tomatoes in half and place in buttered baking dish.
Sprinkle with salt and pepper. Mix butter, parsley and juice
from garlic. Spread over tomatoes, put under grill about
4 inches away from flame. Cook for about 5 minutes, or
until tomatoes begin to get soft and have taken on a nice
colour.

WHOLE FRIED ONIONS

Swedish

4 SERVINGS

8 medium onions
1 pint water
2 oz. margarine

1 teaspoon
brown sugar
salt

Peel and boil onions in lightly salted water for 10 minutes.
Drain, and save $\frac{1}{4}$ pint onion stock. Brown margarine in cast
iron frying pan and add onions. Sprinkle with sugar and
$\frac{1}{2}$ teaspoon salt and brown, shaking the pan to turn them.
Pour in onion stock. Cover and simmer for 30 minutes.
Serve with roast lamb.

STEWED LEEKS

Swedish

4 SERVINGS

4 leeks
½ pint water
2 tablespoons flour

2 oz. butter
¼ pint top of milk
salt

Wash leeks well and cut into ½-inch slices. Place in saucepan with water, butter and a little salt. Boil for about 10 minutes. Mix flour with cold milk and stir into leeks. Simmer for a few minutes, season to taste and serve.

STEWED SPINACH

Swedish

4 SERVINGS

1 large carton frozen chopped spinach
1 oz. butter
5 tablespoons top of milk

½ tablespoon flour
salt

De-frost spinach. Melt butter in a suacepan and stir in flour. Add milk gradually while stirring. Add spinach together with juice which collects when it is de-frosted. Keep on a low flame and stir constantly until it has simmered for a few minutes and has an even creamy consistency. Season to taste. Apart from being served as an ordinary vegetable with fish or meat, this is excellent as a luncheon dish with cold smoked salmon or with scrambled eggs.

STEWED BRUSSELS SPROUTS

Swedish

4 SERVINGS

1½ lb. brussels sprouts
1 pint water
1 bouillon cube
1 oz. butter

1 tablespoon flour
½ teaspoon sugar
1 teaspoon lemon juice

Clean sprouts and drain well. Dissolve bouillon cube in water, add sugar, lemon juice and sprouts. Simmer until sprouts are soft, but just underdone. Melt butter in another saucepan, and stir in flour. Add bouillon gradually while stirring until it has thickened and is smooth. Then add sprouts and let it all come to the boil again. Season if necessary and serve with any meat dish.

BROWNED BRUSSELS SPROUTS

Swedish

4 SERVINGS

1½ lb. brussels sprouts
1 pint water
1 bouillon cube

2 oz. butter
½ teaspoon sugar

Clean sprouts and drain well. Dissolve bouillon cube in water and add sprouts. Simmer until soft. They are best a little underdone. Drain them, and save bouillon for other use. Brown the butter a little in frying pan, add sugar and sprouts. Let sprouts brown on all sides by shaking pan from time to time. Serve with any meat dish.

STEWED WHITE CABBAGE

Swedish

4 SERVINGS

1½ lb. white cabbage
1 oz. butter
½ pint milk

½ tablespoon flour
salt and pepper
water

Clean and dice cabbage, removing stem. Boil in salted water until soft. Drain well. Melt butter in a saucepan and stir in flour. Add milk gradually, stirring continuously until sauce is smooth. Simmer for a few minutes. Add drained cabbage and bring to the boil again. Season to taste and serve with any meat dish.

RED CABBAGE

Danish

6—8 SERVINGS

3 lb. red cabbage
4 tablespoons pork dripping
3 tablespoons vinegar
juice of 1 lemon

4 tablespoons blackcurrant
  juice, undiluted
salt

Remove outer leaves and core of cabbage and cut into half-inch slices. Melt 1 tablespoon dripping and brown about a quarter of the cabbage, season with salt and place in cast iron pot. Continue in the same way until all the cabbage is browned. Add all other ingredients and stir to distribute evenly over cabbage. Cover tightly and simmer for about 60 minutes. Taste and season if necessary. Serve with roast pork or fowl.

STEWED CAULIFLOWER

Swedish

4 SERVINGS

1½ lb. cauliflower	½ tablespoon flour
1 oz. butter	salt and pepper
½ pint milk	water

Clean cauliflower and cut into nice sections, removing coarse stalk. Boil in salted water until just soft. Drain well. Melt butter in a saucepan and stir in flour. Add milk gradually, stirring continuously, until sauce is smooth. Simmer for a few minutes. Add cauliflower and bring to the boil again. Season to taste and serve with any meat dish.

BRUSSELS SPROUTS AND CAULIFLOWER ON MASHED POTATO BED

Swedish

4 SERVINGS

1½ lb. potatoes	4 tablespoons double cream
12 oz. brussels sprouts	2½ oz. butter
12 oz. cauliflower	6 tablespoons milk
½ pint bouillon	salt and pepper

Peel potatoes and put them on to boil. Clean other vegetables and boil them separately in salted water, taking care that they are a little underdone. When potatoes are well done, drain carefully. Melt butter in a saucepan and add milk. Keep on a very low flame. Press potatoes into this, and mash vigorously until white and fluffy. Season with salt and a generous amount of pepper. Drain other vegetables carefully and heat bouillon. Stir in cream. Spread mashed potatoes on a hot serving dish. Place sprouts and cauliflower decoratively on top. Pour sauce over and serve with any meat dish.

EGGS ON SPINACH

Swedish

4 SERVINGS

1 large packet (12 oz.) frozen
    chopped spinach
2 oz. butter
3 tablespoons grated
    Parmesan cheese
4 eggs

2 tablespoons
    breadcrumbs
salt and pepper
cheese sauce
    (see page 68)

De-frost spinach. Make cheese sauce, see page 68. Drain off as much liquid from spinach as possible. Melt butter and stir in spinach. Season to taste with salt and pepper. Pour into shallow, buttered oven dish. Make 4 hollows by pressing with spoon and sprinkle hollows with Parmesan. Break an egg into each hollow. Spoon sauce over eggs and spinach, and sprinkle with breadcrumbs. Bake in heated oven (Regulo 8—475° F.) for about 10 minutes, or until golden brown. Serve with toast.

MIXED VEGETABLES AU GRATIN

Swedish

6 SERVINGS

1 medium cauliflower	$\frac{1}{2}$ pint milk
4 tomatoes	1 egg yolk
6 oz. frozen peas	$\frac{1}{4}$ pint vegetable stock
2 oz. butter	4 tablespoons grated cheese
2 tablespoons flour	salt and pepper

Wash cauliflower and trim off coarse leaves. Boil in slightly salted water until nearly done. Drain well. Butter a large shallow casserole and place cauliflower in centre. Make a ring of de-frosted peas around it. Cut tomatoes in halves and place decoratively around outer edge. Sprinkle with a little salt and pepper. Melt butter in saucepan and stir in flour. Add half pint cauliflower stock gradually whilst stirring. Add milk in same way and stir until smooth and thick. Remove from heat. Beat egg yolk and stir into sauce. Replace on flame and stir until it reaches boiling point. Remove from heat again and stir in cheese. Season to taste with salt and pepper. Pour sauce over vegetables and place in heated oven (Regulo 7—450° F.) for about 12 minutes or until golden brown. Serve immediately.

FRESH SPINACH WITH BUTTER

Swedish

4 SERVINGS

2 lb. spinach	2 oz. butter
salt	

Wash spinach carefully by placing it in a very large bowl so that the leaves float freely. Change water several times to make sure leaves are free of all sand or grit. Place leaves in saucepan and cover tightly. Steam for 5 minutes in the water left on leaves then turn over with 2 forks, cover and steam for another 4 or 5 minutes. Spinach is done when it has turned a dark colour. Drain carefully. Melt butter and stir in about ½ teaspoon salt. Place spinach on heated serving dish, pour butter over it and serve with meat or fish.

MUSHROOM SOUFFLÉ

Swedish

4 SERVINGS

8 oz. mushrooms	3 egg yolks
2 oz. butter	5 egg whites
2 tablespoons flour	1 tablespoon
1 small tin evaporated milk	dry Vermouth
(equivalent to ¾ pint diluted)	water
lemon juice	salt and pepper

Clean and chop mushrooms finely. Sauté in butter for 5 minutes. Season with salt, pepper and a few drops of lemon juice. Sprinkle flour over mushrooms, stir and gradually add tinned milk, diluted with water to make ½ pint in all. Stir until smooth and creamy. Remove from heat. Beat egg yolks and add to cream sauce, beating vigorously. Heat again, stirring until it thickens, but do not boil. Remove from heat, season to taste, stir in Vermouth and set to cool. Beat egg whites until very stiff and fold into sauce. Pour into soufflé pan and bake in heated oven (Regulo 3—350° F.) for 1 hour, or until set. Serve immediately with melted butter.

VEGETABLE SOUFFLÉ

Swedish

4 SERVINGS

¾ pint boiled chopped vegetable
  (asparagus, cauliflower or broccoli)
2 oz. butter
3 tablespoons flour
1 small tin evaporated milk
  (equivalent to ¾ pint diluted)

3 egg yolks
5 egg whites
nutmeg
water
salt and pepper

The vegetable should be slightly underdone and cut into small pieces. Melt butter in saucepan and stir in flour. Dilute tinned milk to make ½ pint in all and add gradually to saucepan, stirring until smooth and creamy. Remove from heat. Beat egg yolk and add to cream sauce, beating vigorously. Heat again whilst stirring until it thickens, but do not boil. Remove from heat, season to taste with salt, pepper and a dash of nutmeg. Stir vegetable into sauce and cool. Beat egg white until very stiff and fold into sauce. Pour into soufflé pan and bake in heated oven (Regulo 3—350° F.) for 1 hour, or until set. Serve immediately with melted butter.

Fish is part of the staple diet for most Scandinavians. Herring, cod and mackerel are abundant in northern waters and there is an unlimited number of recipes for their preparation. But they were not always the most common fish, as this story from Norway illustrates: It appears that some 100 years ago the servants in that country demanded to have a clause put in their employment contract, which stated that it was obligatory to serve something other than salmon on at least one day of the week! But times change and now, I am afraid, salmon is as much a luxury in Scandinavia as it is here.

BAKED MACKEREL WITH HORSERADISH

Swedish

4 SERVINGS

4 mackerel	2 medium tomatoes
4 tablespoons freshly	2 oz. butter
grated horseradish	salt and pepper

Clean and fillet mackerel. Wash and dry fillets and place in buttered casserole. Season with salt and pepper. Sprinkle with horseradish. Slice tomatoes very finely and place in layer over top. Melt butter in saucepan and let it brown a little. Pour over tomatoes, adding salt and pepper to taste. Bake in heated oven (Regulo 7—450° F.) for about 30 minutes. Serve with baked potatoes and green vegetable.

MACKEREL BAKED IN WHITE SAUCE

Swedish

4 SERVINGS

4 mackerel	4 tablespoons chopped dill
2 oz. butter	4 tablespoons breadcrumbs
¾ pint milk	salt and pepper
2 tablespoons flour	

Clean and fillet mackerel. Wash and dry, cut each fillet into 3 pieces and place in buttered casserole. Melt half the butter in saucepan and stir in flour. Add milk gradually, stirring all the time, allowing to come to the boil each time before adding more milk. Season sauce with salt and pepper to taste and let it simmer for a few minutes. Season fish with salt and pepper and sprinkle chopped dill on top. Pour sauce over it and sprinkle breadcrumbs on top. Dot with remainder of butter and bake in heated oven (Regulo 7—450° F.) for about 30 minutes. Serve with boiled potatoes.

BAKED MARINATED MACKEREL

Swedish

4 SERVINGS

4 mackerel
12 tablespoons oil
4 tablespoons lemon juice
1 sachet saffron (5 grains)
½ teaspoon pepper

2 tablespoons chopped chives
2 medium onions
4 medium tomatoes
2 tablespoons chopped dill
salt

Clean and fillet mackerel. Wash and dry them. Mix oil, lemon juice, saffron, pepper and chopped chives and marinate the mackerel fillets in this mixture for at least 1 hour. Wipe casserole with buttered paper, peel and slice onions and place in bottom. Take fillets out of marinade and place in casserole. Sprinkle with a little salt. Slice tomatoes and place on top. Sprinkle with chopped dill. Bake in heated oven (Regulo 7—450° F.) for about 30 minutes. Serve with green salad and potatoes to choice.

FRIED MACKEREL WITH BUTTER SAUCE

Swedish

4 SERVINGS

4 mackerel
3 tablespoons flour
5 tablespoons breadcrumbs
2 medium onions
3 tablespoons vinegar

½ tablespoon ground allspice
4 oz. butter
2 tablespoons chopped parsley
salt
margarine for frying

Clean and fillet mackerel, wash and dry fillets. Mix flour
and breadcrumbs and turn fillets in it so that they are coated
on both sides. Salt lightly and fry golden brown on both
sides. Place on serving dish, keeping warm. Peel onions and
chop finely. Put in small saucepan together with vinegar,
allspice and salt to taste. Cover and let simmer until onion
is transparent. Remove from heat and let it cool a little.
Stir in butter until sauce becomes creamy. Dot this on top
of mackerel, forming a line on each fillet. Sprinkle parsley
on top and serve with mashed potatoes and green salad.

FRIED MACKEREL WITH SOUR CREAM

Swedish

4 SERVINGS

4 mackerel
1 large onion
1 carton sour cream (5 fluid oz.)
4 tablespoons chopped dill

margarine for frying
juice of ½ lemon
breadcrumbs
salt and pepper

Clean and fillet mackerel. Wash and dry fillets. Season with
salt, pepper and lemon juice. Peel and chop onion finely.
Fry golden brown in margarine. Keep warm. Turn fillets

in breadcrumbs and fry in margarine until golden brown. Sprinkle fried onion on top of fried fillets and pour in sour cream. Let it all simmer for 5 minutes. Place in serving dish and sprinkle chopped dill on top. Serve with boiled potatoes.

MACKEREL BAKED IN SOUR CREAM

Swedish

4 SERVINGS

4 mackerels
1 carton sour cream
(5 fluid oz.)
4 tablespoons chopped dill
(or chives)

4 tablespoons breadcrumbs
4 tablespoons grated cheese
salt and pepper

Clean and fillet mackerel. Wash, dry and sprinkle with a little salt and pepper. Place in shallow casserole. Mix sour cream with chopped dill or chives and pour over fish. Mix cheese and breadcrumbs and sprinkle on top. Bake in heated oven (Regulo 7—450° F.) for about 25 minutes. Serve with boiled potatoes and green vegetable.

MOTHER'S MACKEREL CASSEROLE

Swedish

4 SERVINGS

4 mackerel
4 medium tomatoes
2 medium leeks
2 tablespoons chopped dill

$\frac{1}{2}$ teaspoon paprika
juice of $\frac{1}{2}$ lemon
1 carton sour cream (5 fluid oz.)
salt

Clean and fillet mackerel. Wash and dry fillets. Wipe casserole with buttered paper and place fillets in it, with meaty side up. Sprinkle with a little salt. Clean leeks, cut them finely and place on fish. Add chopped tomatoes and dill. Sprinkle paprika on top and add lemon juice and sour cream. Cover and bake in heated oven (Regulo 7—450° F.) for about 30 minutes. Serve with boiled potatoes.

BAKED PAPRIKA MACKEREL

Swedish

4 SERVINGS

4 mackerel
1 medium onion
1 clove garlic
2 teaspoons paprika

1 oz. butter
juice of $\frac{1}{2}$ lemon
1 carton sour cream (5 fluid oz.)
salt

Clean and fillet mackerel. Wash and dry fillets, sprinkle with a little salt. Peel onion and garlic, chop finely and fry golden brown in butter. Stir in paprika. Place mackerel fillets in casserole and pour lemon juice over. Spread fried onion mixture on top and pour sour cream over. Cover casserole and bake in heated oven (Regulo 7—450° F.) for 15 minutes. Remove cover, turn down heat to Regulo 5—400° F. and bake for another 15 minutes. Serve with boiled potatoes.

BAKED MACKEREL WITH STUFFING

Swedish

4 SERVINGS

4 mackerel
2 tablespoons lemon juice
4 slices white bread
4 tablespoons water
4 tablespoons chopped
  parsley

2 tablespoons chopped dill
2 tablespoons chopped chives
3 medium onions
2 tablespoons oil
salt

Clean and fillet mackerel. Wash and dry them, and sprinkle with lemon juice and a little salt. Remove crusts from bread slices and let them soak in water. Peel and chop onions and mix with bread. Stir in chopped dill, parsley and chives and then work in oil. Divide this stuffing into 4 parts and place between each pair of fillets. Wrap the pairs in foil and bake in heated oven (Regulo 7—450° F.) for about 30 minutes. Serve with potatoes boiled with fresh dill.

MACKEREL BAKED IN WINE

Swedish

4 SERVINGS

4 mackerel	2 oz. butter
2 medium onions	6 tablespoons dry white wine
4 medium tomatoes	salt and pepper
2 tablespoons chopped dill	

Clean and fillet mackerel. Wash and dry fillets, sprinkle with a little salt and pepper. Peel onions, slice thinly and fry golden brown in a little of the butter. Place in casserole, covering the bottom. Place mackerel fillets on top, then layer of sliced tomatoes. Sprinkle with chopped dill and dot with remainder of butter. Bake in heated oven (Regulo 7—450° F.) for 15 minutes. Pour wine over it and let it bake for another 10 minutes. Serve with potatoes baked in their jackets.

BAKED MACKEREL WITH LEEKS

Swedish

4 SERVINGS

4 mackerel	3 tablespoons vinegar
2 medium onions	9 tablespoons oil
2 leeks	2 tablespoons chopped dill
sprigs of dill	salt

Clean and fillet mackerel. Wash and dry fillets, sprinkle with a little salt. Wipe casserole with buttered paper and place fillets in it, meaty side up. Peel and chop onions and leeks. Mix together and place in layer over fish. Put a few sprigs of dill on top of this. Mix oil and vinegar and pour

over this. Cover dish and bake in heated oven (Regulo
7—450° F.) for about 30 minutes. When dish is ready,
remove sprigs of dill and sprinkle with freshly chopped
dill instead. Serve with potatoes baked in their jackets.

BAKED MACKEREL WITH CARROTS

Swedish

4 SERVINGS

4 mackerel	1 tablespoon brown sugar
8 oz. carrots	2 oz. butter
2 tablespoons French mustard	4 tablespoons breadcrumbs
6 tablespoons mayonnaise	salt and pepper
2 medium onions	

Clean and fillet mackerel. Wash, dry and sprinkle with
a little salt. Butter large, shallow oven dish, place fillets
in it. Mix mustard and mayonnaise and spread over fish.
Chop onions finely and sprinkle on top. Season with a little
pepper. Clean and slice carrots, place in a ring around
mackerel. Melt butter and pour over carrots. Sprinkle
carrots with brown sugar. Bake in heated oven (Regulo
7—450° F.) for about 25 minutes. Sprinkle breadcrumbs
over it and let it bake for another 5 minutes. Serve with
boiled potatoes and green salad.

MARINATED AND FRIED MACKEREL

Swedish

4 SERVINGS

4 mackerel	1 tablespoon salt
sprigs of dill	½ tablespoon sugar
1 tablespoon chopped onion	pepper
¼ pint vinegar	margarine for frying

Clean and fillet mackerel. Wash and dry fillets. Place 4 fillets in a bowl large enough to hold them side by side, leaving meaty side up. Place generous amount of dill sprigs on this and sprinkle with chopped onion and quite a lot of pepper. Place other fillets on top, meaty side down. Mix vinegar, salt and sugar and pour over fish. Let it marinate overnight. Remove fillets from marinade, wipe them off and fry in margarine. Place on hot serving dish. Rinse out frying pan with 4—5 tablespoons of marinade and pour over fish. Serve with mashed potatoes.

FRIED MACKEREL WITH TOMATOES

Swedish

4 SERVINGS

4 mackerel	margarine for frying
1 egg	mayonnaise
8 medium tomatoes	chopped dill
breadcrumbs	salt and pepper

Clean and fillet mackerel, wash and dry fillets. Beat egg and dip fillets in it. Mix some breadcrumbs with salt and pepper to taste and turn fillets in this. Fry golden brown and keep warm. Slice tomatoes and fry in margarine. Sprinkle with a little salt and pepper. Place bed of fried tomatoes on hot serving dish, keeping back 8 slices. Put fried fillets on tomato bed, and garnish each fillet with remaining slices. Mix mayonnaise with as much chopped dill as needed to turn it green and serve in sauce bowl. Baked potatoes go well with this.

FRIED MACKEREL
WITH ANCHOVY STUFFING

Swedish

4 SERVINGS

4 mackerel	10 anchovy fillets
juice of $\frac{1}{2}$ lemon	1 tablespoon chopped chives
1 teaspoon ground allspice	1 tablespoon chopped parsley
1 egg	$\frac{1}{2}$ oz. butter
breadcrumbs	sliced lemon for garnish
margarine for frying	salt
2 hard-boiled eggs	

Clean and fillet mackerel. Wash and dry fillets. Sprinkle allspice and a little salt over fillets and let them stand for 10 minutes. Beat egg, dip in fillets, turn them in bread-crumbs and fry golden brown in margarine. Place in pairs on serving dish and keep warm. Chop anchovy fillets finely and mash together with hard-boiled eggs, using a fork. Mix in chopped parsley and chives and lightly fry in butter. Spread filling on 4 of the fillets, placing other 4 on top. Garnish with lemon slices and serve with mashed potatoes and creamed spinach.

FRIED MACKEREL WITH TOMATO
AND MUSHROOM SAUCE

Swedish

4 SERVINGS

4 mackerel
4 peeled tomatoes
4 oz. mushrooms
3 medium onions
3 oz. butter

1 clove garlic
4 tablespoons flour
4 tablespoons breadcrumbs
margarine for frying
salt and pepper

Clean and fillet mackerel, wash, dry and sprinkle with a little salt and pepper. Peel and chop onion and let it sauté in saucepan together with sliced mushrooms, chopped tomatoes and crushed garlic. Season to taste, cover and let it simmer. Mix flour and breadcrumbs and turn fillets in this. Fry them golden brown and place on hot serving dish. When mackerel is done, so is tomato and mushroom sauce, which is then poured over fish. Serve with mashed potatoes.

FRIED MACKEREL WITH CAPERS

Swedish

4 SERVINGS

4 mackerel
1 tablespoon capers
top of the milk
1½ teaspoons soya sauce
1 lemon

breadcrumbs
margarine for frying
salt

Clean and fillet mackerel. Wash and dry fillets. Sprinkle with a little salt, turn them in breadcrumbs and fry golden brown in margarine. Place on serving dish and keep warm. Add capers, soya sauce and top of the milk to margarine that is left in pan and bring to the boil. Pour sauce over mackerel. Chop lemon with peel and sprinkle on top. Serve with mashed potatoes and green salad.

STUFFED FILLET OF MACKEREL

Swedish

4 SERVINGS

4 medium mackerel, filleted
6 oz. mushrooms
1 oz. butter
1 tablespoon Worcester sauce

½ tablespoon chopped, fresh dill
½ tablespoon chopped chives
tomatoes and parsley for garnish

Soak fish fillets in cold, salted water (3 tablespoons to 2 pints water) for 10—15 minutes. Remove fish, dry it, discarding water. Chop mushrooms finely, but do not wash and peel them. Melt butter in saucepan and let mushrooms sauté slowly for a few minutes until soft. Remove from heat and allow to cool a little before mixing in other ingredients. Divide mixture in 4 portions and spread over 4 of the fillets. Place other 4 fillets on top, pressing them together in pairs. Wrap each pair in tin foil, place in oven dish and bake in heated oven (Regulo 7—450° F.) for 20—25 minutes. Remove fish from wrapping, place on hot serving dish and pour juice over them. Garnish with quartered tomatoes and chopped parsley and serve with boiled potatoes and green salad.

MUSTARD MACKEREL

Swedish

4 SERVINGS

4 mackerel	5 tablespoons breadcrumbs
sliced cheese	salt
French mustard	margarine for frying
3 tablespoons flour	

Clean and fillet mackerel. Wash and dry them and cut each fillet in 2 pieces. Put pairs of mackerel pieces together with slice of cheese and mustard to taste between them. Mix flour and breadcrumbs together and turn pieces in it so that they are coated on each side. Sprinkle with a little salt and fry golden brown. Serve with boiled rice and green salad.

BOILED MACKEREL TO BE SERVED COLD

Swedish

4—6 SERVINGS

4 medium mackerel	4 white peppercorns
2 pints water	5 allspice corns
3 tablespoons vinegar	1 bay leaf
1 tablespoon salt	fresh dill

Clean and trim mackerel in usual way, making sure it is carefully washed. Allow to soak in cold salted water (3 tablespoons salt to 2 pints water) for 15—20 minutes. Remove mackerel and discard water. Put 2 pints water in fish kettle and add all spices except dill. Bring to the boil. Place mackerel on grating and cover with fresh dill. Lower gently into boiling water, which should just cover fish. Bring to the boil again and skim off any foam. Reduce heat, cover and allow to simmer for 10—15 minutes, depending on size. Test with fork to see when done. Place fish in suitable bowl, strain liquid over it and set to cool. Before serving chill well, discard liquid and garnish with fresh dill. Serve with strong fish sauce and salad.

HERRING OR MACKEREL CASSEROLE

Swedish

4 SERVINGS

2 lb. herring or mackerel	$\frac{1}{2}$ tablespoon chopped chives
1 teaspoon salt	
$\frac{1}{4}$ teaspoon pepper	5 tablespoons vinegar
$\frac{1}{2}$ teaspoon crushed cloves	1 tablespoon butter
1 tablespoon chopped parsley	breadcrumbs

Prepare casserole by wiping it with buttered paper and coating with breadcrumbs. Fillet fish and let it soak in cold, salted water (3 tablespoons salt to 2 pints water) for 10 minutes. Remove fillets, discarding water, and let them drain well. Score skin of each fillet a couple of times. Roll each fillet up and place in casserole so that they stand close together. Sprinkle spices on top. Pour vinegar over it and dot with butter. Place in heated oven (Regulo 8—475° F.) and bake for 10 minutes. Take out casserole and sprinkle top with breadcrumbs. Then bake for another 10 minutes, when it should be ready to be served with fried or boiled new potatoes.

FRIED HERRING WITH ONION SAUCE

Swedish

4 SERVINGS

4 herrings, filleted
rye or wholemeal flour
margarine for frying
1 oz. butter
2 tablespoons flour

1 pint milk
2 medium onions
1 teaspoon cold butter
salt and pepper

Soak fish fillets in cold, salted water (3 tablespoons salt to 2 pints water) for 10—15 minutes. Drain them and discard water. Turn fillets in wholemeal flour and fry golden brown on each side. Place on a serving dish and keep warm in oven. Peel and chop onions. Brown the butter in frying pan and fry onions golden brown. Sprinkle flour on top and stir in. Add milk gradually, stirring constantly and letting sauce thicken before adding more milk, until it is all worked in. Season to taste, cover and let sauce simmer for 10 minutes. Remove from heat and stir in cold butter. Pour sauce over fish and serve with potatoes baked in their jackets.

PARTY HERRING

Swedish

4 SERVINGS

4 herrings
6 tablespoons oil
6 tablespoons tomato purée
10 allspice

4 medium onions
2 tablespoons vinegar
½ tablespoon sugar
salt

Clean and fillet herrings. Sprinkle fillets with a little salt and roll them up separately. Place in saucepan. Peel and slice onions and place on top of rolled herring fillets. Mix all other ingredients and pour over. Cover and let it simmer on low heat for about 20 minutes, or until onion is transparent. Serve with potatoes boiled with fresh dill.

FRIED HERRING WITH CURRY SAUCE

Swedish

4 SERVINGS

4 herrings
2 medium onions
2 medium apples
1 teaspoon curry powder
1 carton single cream
  (2·7 fluid oz.)

1 tablespoon chopped parsley
4 tablespoons breadcrumbs
2 tablespoons plain flour
salt and pepper
margarine for frying

Clean and fillet herrings, season with salt and pepper. Mix breadcrumbs and flour and turn fillets in this. Fry golden brown in margarine. Place on hot serving dish and keep warm. Chop onions finely and fry golden brown. Peel apples and dice rather finely. When onion is brown, take frying pan off flame and mix in apples, curry powder and a little salt. Replace on low flame and stir in cream. Bring almost to the boil and pour over herrings. Sprinkle with chopped parsley and serve with mashed potatoes.

WEST COAST HERRING CASSEROLE

Swedish

4 SERVINGS

6 salted herring fillets
8 oz. carrots
2 medium leeks

1 carton sour cream
(5 fluid oz.)
2 oz. butter
2 tablespoons breadcrumbs

Soak herring fillets in cold water overnight. Remove skins.
Butter a casserole. Dry herring fillets and cut them diagonally
across into inch-wide strips. Place in casserole. Clean and
slice carrots, place on top of herrings. Clean leeks and slice
crosswise. Place in layer on top of carrots. Dot butter on
top of this and pour cream over. Sprinkle with breadcrumbs,
and bake in heated oven (Regulo 5—400° F.) for about
45 minutes. Serve with mashed potatoes.

BAKED HERRING WITH MUSSELS

Swedish

4 SERVINGS

4 fresh herrings
1 tin mussels (5 oz.)
chopped dill
2 tablespoons breadcrumbs

2 oz. butter
1 carton single cream
(2·7 fluid oz.)
salt and pepper

Clean and fillet herrings. Butter an oven dish and place
4 fillets side by side in it, skin side down. Season with
salt and pepper. Fry mussels lightly in half the butter and
spread on top of herrings. Sprinkle generously with chopped
dill. Place remaining 4 fillets on top, skin side up. Sprinkle

breadcrumbs over them and dot with rest of butter. Bake in heated oven (Regulo 7—450° F.) for 15 minutes. Pour cream over and bake for another 10 minutes. Serve with mashed or boiled potatoes and green vegetable.

BAKED HERRING WITH ANCHOVY SAUCE

Swedish

4 SERVINGS

4 herrings
8 anchovy fillets
1 carton single cream
  (2·7 fluid oz.)

3 tablespoons breadcrumbs
1 oz. butter
salt, pepper and lemon juice

Clean and fillet herrings. Butter shallow oven dish and place fillets in it, skin side down. Season with salt, pepper and a little lemon juice. Chop anchovy fillets finely and mix into cream. Spread this over herring. Sprinkle with breadcrumbs and dot butter on top. Bake in heated oven (Regulo 7—450° F.) for about 30 minutes. Serve with mashed potatoes.

HERRING WITH ONIONS

Swedish

4 SERVINGS

4 herrings
4 medium onions
1 egg
6 tablespoons breadcrumbs

4 oz. margarine
1 carton single cream
(2·7 fluid oz.)
salt and pepper

Clean and fillet herrings. Season with salt and pepper. Peel
and slice onions. Fry golden brown in some of the margarine.
Place 4 fillets, skin side down, on a board. Put fried onions
on top of 4 fillets and cover with remaining fillets, skin
side up. Press them down so that each pair holds together.
Beat egg and dip each herring pair in it, after which it is
turned in breadcrumbs and fried in margarine until golden
brown on each side. Place in shallow oven dish. Bring cream
to the boil and pour over herrings. Place in heated oven
(Regulo 5—400° F.) for 5 minutes. Serve with boiled or
mashed potatoes.

KNUT'S HERRING CASSEROLE

Swedish

4 SERVINGS

4 herrings
3 oz. butter
2 tablespoons grated
horseradish
5 tablespoons cream

2 tablespoons tomato purée
3 tablespoons water
3 tablespoons breadcrumbs
salt

Clean and fillet herrings. Season with a little salt. Mix
butter and grated horse-radish to a paste and divide between

fillets, putting a little on each. Roll fillets up and place in buttered oven dish. Mix tomato purée, water and cream together and pour over fish. Sprinkle breadcrumbs on top and bake in heated oven (Regulo 5—400° F.) for about 30 minutes. Serve with boiled potatoes.

STUFFED HERRING

Swedish

4 SERVINGS

4 large herrings	4 tablespoons chopped onions
2 tablespoons butter	2 tablespoons lemon juice
8 tablespoons chopped parsley	pepper
4 tablespoons chopped chives	parsley and lemon for garnish

Clean fish and trim off fins. Wash carefully in cold water. Soak fish in cold, salted water (3 tablespoons salt to 2 pints water) for 10—15 minutes. Remove fish and dry it, discarding water. Mix all ingredients, divide into 4 parts and stuff a portion inside flaps of each fish. Wrap fish separately in tin foil and place packages side by side in oven pan. Cook in heated oven (Regulo 7—450° F.) for 25—30 minutes. Remove fish from their wrappings and place on hot serving dish. Pour juice from wrapping over them, garnish with sliced lemon and sprigs of parsley. Serve with boiled potatoes and green salad.

MARGARETA HERRING

Swedish

4 SERVINGS

4 large herrings
2 oz. butter
4 tablespoons French mustard

4 tablespoons tomato purée
4 tablespoons cream
salt

Clean, wash and fillet herrings. Divide butter equally between 8 fillets, place some on each one and roll them up separately, with skin side out. Pack into casserole and sprinkle with a little salt. Mix mustard, tomato purée and cream to a smooth sauce and spread over fish. Bake in heated oven (Regulo 5—400° F.) for about 30 minutes. Serve with mashed potatoes.

MARSTRAND'S HERRING

Swedish

4 SERVINGS

4 large herrings
8 small onions
½ oz. butter
juice of ½ lemon
4 tablespoons chopped dill

4 tablespoons cream
4 crushed cloves
1 crushed bay leaf
salt

Clean, wash and fillet herrings. Peel onions and put in saucepan with ¼ pint water and butter. Allow to simmer until onions are soft. Place herring fillets in wide saucepan with a little salt, and add onions with their water. Add lemon juice and cream, sprinkle dill and spices on top. Liquid should come about half way up contents. Cover tightly and bring to the boil. Turn heat down and allow to simmer for 15 minutes. Serve with mashed potatoes.

FISH CAKES MADE FROM FRESH HERRINGS

Swedish

4 SERVINGS

1½ lb. herrings
2 medium boiled potatoes
2 tablespoons chopped onions

1 tablespoon butter
salt and pepper
oil for deep frying

Fillet herrings and remove all bones that might be left. Pass fish and potatoes through mincer. Fry chopped onion lightly in butter and add to mince. Mix well and season to taste. Form mixture into cakes and deep fry them. Serve with boiled potatoes and currant sauce (see page 70).

GRANDMOTHER'S HERRING

Swedish

4 SERVINGS

6 salted herring fillets
2 hard-boiled eggs
2 oz. butter

2 tablespoons chopped
  parsley
2 leeks, finely chopped

Soak herring fillets overnight in cold water. Remove skin and dice rather finely. Place herrings in saucepan and add sufficient water barely to cover them. Bring to the boil. Chop eggs finely and add fish, together with butter. Allow to simmer for a few minutes and add parsley and chopped leeks. When leeks are cooked, dish is ready to serve with boiled potatoes.

STEAMED HERRING WITH BOILED POTATOES

Swedish

4 SERVINGS

4—6 salted herring fillets	dill
2 hard-boiled eggs	potatoes
2 oz. butter	

Soak herrings overnight in cold water. Remove skins and dry them. Peel sufficient potatoes for 4 servings and boil in saucepan in usual way. Choose serving dish that fits on top of saucepan and place herrings in it. Chop hard-boiled eggs and sprinkle on top of herring, together with some chopped fresh dill. Dot butter on top and cover. Serve when potatoes are cooked.

BOILED HERRING FOR SERVING COLD

Swedish

4 SERVINGS

4 herrings	½ medium onion
¾ pint vinegar	1 clove garlic
½ pint water	½ medium carrot
1 bay leaf	1 teaspoon salt

Put all the ingredients except herrings in fish kettle and allow to boil for ½ hour. Clean and trim herrings in usual way, making sure they are carefully washed. Allow to soak in cold salted water (3 tablespoons salt to 2 pints water) for 10—15 minutes. Remove fish and discard water. Make

3 scores on sides of each fish, place on grating and lower gently into marinade. Allow to simmer for about 10 minutes, watching carefully as they easily fall apart if boiled too long. Place herrings in suitable bowl, strain marinade over them and set to cool. Serve with boiled new potatoes and salad.

POTATOES STUFFED WITH HERRING

Swedish

4 SERVINGS

2 salted herring fillets	1 egg yolk
8 medium potatoes	2 tablespoons
2 medium onions	double cream
1 oz. butter	pepper

Soak herring fillets overnight in cold water. Remove skins, dry and chop finely. Peel potatoes and parboil them. Peel onions, chop finely and fry lightly in butter. Slice off a piece of each potato, so that they can stand up on end. Scoop out about half of each one. Chop this up and mix with onions, herring, egg yolk and cream. Season to taste with pepper. Butter an oven dish, stand potatoes in it and stuff with mixture. Bake in heated oven (Regulo 5—400° F.) for 15—20 minutes. Serve with green salad.

COBBLER'S HERRING

Swedish

4 SERVINGS

8 salted herring fillets
2 tablespoons vinegar
2 bay leaves

3 oz. butter
1 tablespoon chopped parsley
1 teaspoon lemon juice

Soak herring fillets overnight in cold water. Remove skins and roll each fillet up, securing with a tooth pick. Boil in water to which vinegar and bay leaves are added for 10—15 minutes. Melt butter and add lemon juice. Place herrings on warm dish, sprinkle parsley over them and pour melted butter on top. Serve steaming hot with boiled potatoes.

HERRING AND LEEK CASSEROLE

Swedish

4 SERVINGS

6 salted herring fillets
6 leeks
2 oz. butter

3 tablespoons grated cheese
5 tablespoons top of the milk

Soak herring fillets in cold water overnight. Remove skins and dry. Clean leeks carefully and parboil them. Cut into halves. Butter a casserole. Place 2 pieces of leek on each fillet and roll them up. Place standing on their sides in casserole. Dot butter on top, sprinkle with cheese and pour milk over. Bake in heated oven (Regulo 5—400° F.) for about 45 minutes. Serve with mashed potatoes.

CRAYFISH

Swedish

4 SERVINGS

40 live crayfish   5 tablespoons salt
8 pints water   plenty of fresh dill

Wash live crayfish in cold water. Put water to boil in large pot and add salt and dill. When water is boiling rapidly, plunge crayfish into it head first, one by one. If boiling slows down, pause until it is boiling rapidly again before adding more crayfish. When all are in, turn down flame, cover and boil for 6 minutes. Remove from heat and set to cool in own stock. When cold, arrange crayfish decoratively on large serving dish, garnish with fresh dill crowns and chill before serving with toast and butter.

WHITING BAKED WITH VEGETABLES

Norwegian

4 SERVINGS

2 lb. whiting   6 tablespoons white wine
3 leeks   3 oz. margarine
2 carrots   2 tablespoons grated cheese
juice of 1 lemon   2 tablespoons breadcrumbs
6 tablespoons sour cream   salt and pepper

Fillet the whiting, wash and dry it. Clean the vegetables and slice them. Butter a casserole and put the fish and vegetables in alternate layers in it. Season between the layers with salt, pepper and lemon juice. Pour the white wine and sour cream over and sprinkle the cheese and breadcrumbs on top. Dot with the margarine and bake in pre-heated oven (Regulo 7—450° F.) for about 35 minutes. Serve with potatoes to choice.

WHITING BAKED WITH MUSTARD

Norwegian

4 SERVINGS

2 lb. whiting
3 tablespoons chopped onion
1 tablespoon French mustard
4 oz. margarine

2 tablespoons grated cheese
2 tablespoons breadcrumbs
salt and pepper

Fillet the whiting, wash and dry it. Place fillets in a buttered casserole. Season with salt and pepper. Melt margarine and let chopped onion simmer in it until transparent. Stir in mustard. Pour this sauce over fish. Sprinkle cheese and breadcrumbs on top and bake in pre-heated oven (Regulo 7—450° F.) for 30 minutes. Serve with mashed potatoes and green salad.

WHITING BAKED WITH TOMATOES

Norwegian

4 SERVINGS

2 lb. whiting
2 tablespoons lemon juice
2 medium onions
2 medium tomatoes

2 oz. butter
2 tablespoons breadcrumbs
salt

Fillet the whiting, wash and dry it. Place fillets in buttered casserole. Season with salt and lemon juice. Peel and chop onions finely. Fry them golden brown in half the butter and sprinkle over fish. Slice tomatoes and place in layer on top. Sprinkle breadcrumbs over it and dot with rest of butter. Bake in pre-heated oven (Regulo 7—450° F.) for 30 minutes. Serve with mashed potatoes and green salad.

STEWED WHITING

Norwegian

4 SERVINGS

2 lb. whiting
½ pint water
3 tablespoons flour

4 tablespoons chopped chives
salt

Fillet fish and wash fillets, heads and bones. Boil heads and bones in ½ pint water for 15 minutes, to make stock. Strain stock. Stir flour in a little water and add to stock while stirring. Let it simmer for a few minutes and season with salt and chopped chives. Put fillets in sauce and let them simmer for about 10 minutes. Serve with boiled potatoes and a vegetable.

STEWED FISH

Norwegian

4 SERVINGS

1 lb. boiled fish
1 lb. boiled potatoes
1 oz. butter
2 tablespoons flour

¾ pint milk
nutmeg
salt and pepper

This dish is often made with leftovers, in which case quantities should be adjusted to above proportions. Bone fish carefully and separate it into little pieces. Dice potatoes rather finely. Melt butter in saucepan and stir in flour. Add hot milk gradually, stirring all the time so that sauce becomes smooth. Add fish and potatoes, season with salt, pepper and nutmeg. Allow to simmer for 10 minutes, when it is ready to be served.

FISH PUDDING WITH MUSHROOM SAUCE

Norwegian

6 SERVINGS

3 lb. haddock fillet
1 tablespoon potato flour
1 tablespoon plain flour
4 oz. butter

3 pints milk
1 tablespoon salt
½ teaspoon pepper

Remove skin and bones from fillets. Mince fish and place in a large bowl. Add flour, salt, pepper and butter. Pound it all together, using a wooden spoon. Keep pounding for about 20 minutes, when mixture should be perfectly smooth, like a paste. Add milk very gradually while stirring, starting with no more than 2 tablespoons at a time. Butter a suitable oven dish and put mixture in it. Bake in pre-heated oven (Regulo 5—400° F.) for 45—60 minutes. Serve with mushroom sauce (see page 70).

BRAISED FISH FILLET WITH CREAM SAUCE

Swedish

4 SERVINGS

1½ lb. fish fillet to choice
1½ tablespoons butter
1 carton single cream
    (2.7 fluid oz.)

1 tablespoon tomato purée
or 4 oz. shrimps
or 4 oz. mushrooms
salt and pepper

Butter a suitable oven dish, season fillets lightly on both sides and place side by side in dish. If using tomato purée, stir it into cream and pour over fish. If shrimps are used, just place them on top of fish and pour cream over. If mushrooms are used, they should be sliced and fried lightly in some butter before being placed on fish. Cover with lid or buttered paper and allow to poach in pre-heated oven (Regulo 7—450° F.) for about 10 minutes. Serve directly with boiled potatoes or rice and green vegetable.

BRAISED FISH STEAKS

Swedish

4 SERVINGS

4 fish steaks (cod or haddock)	white wine
2 tablespoons butter	chopped parsley
1 medium onion	salt and pepper

Choose an oven dish just large enough to hold fish steaks side by side. Spread butter thickly over bottom and sides. Peel and chop onion and spread over bottom of dish. Lightly salt and pepper fish steaks on both sides and place in dish. Sprinkle chopped parsley on top and pour in sufficient wine to come half way up fish. Cover with lid or buttered paper. Allow to poach in pre-heated oven (Regulo 7—450° F.) for about 10 minutes. Serve with mashed potatoes and vegetable to choice.

BAKED COD IN TOMATO SAUCE

Norwegian

4 SERVINGS

1½ lb. cod fillet	2 tablespoons lemon juice
1 medium onion	2 teaspoons French mustard
6 tablespoons water	1 oz. butter
6 tablespoons tomato purée	salt

Wash and dry cod fillets. Place in a shallow, buttered oven dish side by side. Season with salt. Chop onion finely and fry golden brown in butter. Add tomato purée, mustard and water, stirring until smooth. Allow to simmer a few minutes. Add lemon juice and season to taste with salt. Pour sauce over cod and bake in pre-heated oven (Regulo 7—450° F.) for about 30 minutes. Serve with boiled potatoes.

COD AND POTATO CASSEROLE

Norwegian

4 SERVINGS

1½ lb. cod fillet	3 tablespoons breadcrumbs
6 medium potatoes	2 oz. butter
1 medium onion	salt and pepper
2 tablespoons chopped parsley	lemon juice

Wash and dry cod fillets. Butter a shallow oven dish and place fillets side by side in it. Sprinkle with lemon juice, salt and pepper to taste. Peel and slice potatoes, place in a layer over cod. Dot with butter and bake in pre-heated oven (Regulo 7—450° F.) for 15 minutes. Peel and chop onion.

Sprinkle over potatoes together with parsley and bread-crumbs. Bake for another 15 minutes. Serve with green vegetable or salad.

COD BAKED IN MAYONNAISE

Norwegian

4 SERVINGS

1½ lb. cod fillet
1 onion
2 tablespoons chopped parsley

10 tablespoons mayonnaise
salt and pepper
3 tablespoons breadcrumbs

Wash and dry cod fillets. Place in a buttered casserole and season with salt and pepper. Sprinkle parsley over it and then cover with mayonnaise. Bake in pre-heated oven, (Regulo 7—450° F.) for 20 minutes. Sprinkle breadcrumbs over it and bake another 5 minutes. Serve with mashed potatoes.

BAKED COD A LA PER

Norwegian

4 SERVINGS

1½ lb. cod fillet
3 tablespoons chopped parsley
1 medium onion

2 oz. butter
3 tablespoons breadcrumbs
salt and lemon juice

Chop onion and mix with parsley. Spread over the bottom of a buttered oven dish. Wash and dry cod fillets. Place over chopped onion and dot butter on top. Sprinkle with salt and breadcrumbs and bake in pre-heated oven (Regulo 7—450° F.) for about 30 minutes. Squeeze some lemon juice over before serving with mashed potatoes.

BAKED COD WITH CHEESE

Norwegian

4 SERVINGS

1½ lb. cod fillet   salt and pepper
sliced cheese

Rinse and dry fillets. Butter a shallow oven dish and place
fillets side by side in it. Season with salt and pepper. Cover
fish with sliced cheese. Place in pre-heated oven (Regulo
7—450° F.) for about 20 minutes, when cod should be
cooked. Then place under grill until cheese becomes light
brown and crisp. Serve with baked potatoes and green salad.

COD STEW

Norwegian

4 SERVINGS

1 lb. cod fillet   4 medium carrots
½ lb. brussels sprouts   1 pint milk
½ celeriac   1 oz. butter
1 leek   2 tablespoons flour
4 medium potatoes   4 tablespoons chopped parsley

Clean, peel and dice all vegetables into about ½-inch cubes.
Place in a saucepan, season and boil in milk. Wash cod fillets
and place in a colander that fits into saucepan. Cover tightly
and leave to steam until vegetables are cooked. Strain off
milk. Cut cod into pieces and mix with vegetables. Melt
butter in another saucepan and stir in flour. Add milk
gradually, stirring until sauce is smooth. Allow to simmer

for 10 minutes. Season with salt and pepper and stir in chopped parsley. Pour sauce over fish and vegetables. Mix all together and allow to come to boil again, after which it is ready to be served.

COD WITH RICE AND TOMATO SAUCE

Norwegian

4 SERVINGS

3 cups boiled cod (leftover)
3 cups boiled rice
1 tablespoon flour
2 oz. margarine
½ pint milk

2 tablespoons tomato purée
2 tablespoons breadcrumbs
sugar
salt and pepper

Shred and bone fish carefully. Place fish and rice in layers in a casserole. Melt half the margarine in saucepan and stir in flour. Add milk gradually while stirring until sauce is smooth. Stir in tomato purée. Season to taste with salt, pepper and a little sugar. Pour sauce over fish. Sprinkle breadcrumbs on top and dot with rest of butter. Place in pre-heated oven (Regulo 7—450° F.) for about 30 minutes. Serve with green salad.

POACHED COD

Norwegian

4 SERVINGS

1½ lb. cod steaks
1 oz. margarine
sliced lemon

chopped parsley
salt and pepper

Wash and dry cod steaks. Melt margarine in wide saucepan and place cod steaks in it, side by side. Season with salt and pepper. Place lemon slice on each cod steak and sprinkle chopped parsley on top. Cover tightly and allow to poach on low heat for about 15 minutes. Shake saucepan from time to time, to make sure fish does not stick to bottom. Serve with its natural sauce and mashed potatoes.

STEAMED COD WITH CHEESE SAUCE

Norwegian

4 SERVINGS

1½ lb. cod fillet
½ tablespoon salt
1 tablespoon vinegar
6 peppercorns
1 leek
2 oz. butter

2 tablespoons flour
½ pint milk
4 tablespoons grated
  cheese
4 servings potatoes
salt and pepper

Prepare potatoes and place in water to boil. Fit a casserole on top and allow to get warm. Wash cod fillets and rub with mixture of salt and vinegar. Place in casserole. Sprinkle peppercorns on top. Clean leek carefully and slice finely. Place on top of fish and dot with half the butter. Cover tightly and fish should be ready at the same time as potatoes.

To make sauce mix flour with a little milk. Bring remainder of milk to the boil and stir in flour mixture. Pour stock which collects in casserole into saucepan containing sauce and allow to simmer for 5 minutes. Add remainder of butter and cheese. Allow to simmer for another 5 minutes, season to taste with salt and pepper. When fish and potatoes are done, sauce can either be poured into casserole or served separately.

BOILED COD WITH MUSTARD SAUCE

Norwegian

4 SERVINGS

1½ lb. cod steak	½ pint fish stock
2 pints water	1 oz. butter
2 tablespoons salt	3 teaspoons French
1 tablespoon vinegar	mustard
2 tablespoons flour	lemon slices
½ pint milk	salt and pepper

Allow cod steaks to rinse in running water while sauce is prepared. Make stock by boiling some fish scraps. Stir flour in a little milk. Bring remainder of milk and fish stock to the boil and stir in flour mixture. Let sauce simmer for 10 minutes. Add butter and mustard and season to taste with salt and pepper. While sauce is simmering, put on water for cod and bring to the boil with salt and vinegar added. Put in cod steaks and when it comes to the boil again, skim off any foam. Allow to simmer for about 10 minutes, when cod should be ready to be served, decorated with lemon slices. Serve sauce separately. Boiled potatoes and a cooked vegetable go well with this.

COD A LA TRONDHEIM

Norwegian

4 SERVINGS

1½ lb. cod fillet
2 carrots
½ celeriac (or ½ cup diced
  celery)
3 tablespoons chopped parsley

1 medium onion
6 slices white bread
3 oz. butter
3 tablespoons breadcrumbs
salt and pepper

Peel and grate carrots and celeriac. Chop onion finely. Remove edges of bread and cut up in little cubes. Melt butter. Mix vegetables, bread and parsley in a bowl with melted butter, and season to taste with salt and pepper. Wash cod fillets and dry them. Place in shallow buttered oven dish and season with salt. Spread vegetable mixture over fish and sprinkle breadcrumbs on top. Bake in pre-heated oven (Regulo 7—450° F.) for about 30 minutes. Serve with potatoes to choice.

BAKED COD WITH APPLES AND CELERIAC

Norwegian

4 SERVINGS

1½ lb. cod fillet
½ celeriac (or ½ cup diced
  celery)
4 medium cooking apples

1 medium onion
4 tablespoons tomato purée
¼ pint top of the milk
salt and pepper

Peel onion, apples and celeriac and chop finely. Mix together and spread in bottom of a shallow, buttered oven dish. Wash and dry cod fillets and place on top. Season with salt and pepper to taste. Mix milk and tomato purée into a sauce and pour over fish. Bake in pre-heated oven (Regulo 7—450° F.) for about 30 minutes. Serve with boiled potatoes.

BOILED COD OR HADDOCK STEAKS

Swedish

4—6 SERVINGS

2 lb. cod or haddock steaks   1 slice of onion
2 pints water   parsley
2 tablespoons salt   lemon

Make desired sauce before boiling fish, see pages 68—70. Place fish steaks in cold, salted water (3 tablespoons salt to 2 pints water) for 10 minutes. Meantime, bring water, salt and onion slice to the boil in fish kettle. Take fish out of cold water, which is discarded, place steaks carefully on grating and sink into water. There should be just enough to cover fish. Bring to the boil again and skim off any foam. Cover and simmer for about 5 minutes, when meat should just have loosened from bone. Be careful not to overcook fish as it then loses its flavour. As water in which fish is boiled is very salty, it should not be used as stock for sauce. Place fish steaks on hot serving dish, garnish with slices of lemon and chopped parsley, serve immediately with boiled or mashed potatoes. Any of the following sauces would be suitable: caper sauce, lemon sauce or shrimp sauce.

SMOKED COD WITH GRATED CARROTS

Norwegian

4 SERVINGS

1½ lb. smoked cod fillet
3 tablespoons oil
4 oz. butter

1 tablespoon lemon juice
2 tablespoons chopped parsley
2 teaspoons French mustard

Wash and dry smoked cod fillets. Cut them into suitable portions. Put oil in frying pan and turn fillets in it. Fry on a low flame, shaking pan from time to time. Flame should be low enough to cook fillets through without browning them. When ready, place them on a hot serving dish and spread a little mustard on each piece. This is best done with a brush, to get it evenly spread in a thin layer. While fish is still frying, mix butter, lemon juice and parsley together into a smooth paste. Dot each piece of cod with this before serving with raw grated carrots and mashed potatoes.

SMOKED COD BAKED WITH TOMATOES

Norwegian

4 SERVINGS

1½ lb. smoked cod fillet
6 medium tomatoes
2 oz. butter
1 tablespoon chopped onion

6 tablespoons boiling water
1 tablespoon chopped parsley
2 tablespoons breadcrumbs
oil

Wash and dry cod fillets. Cut them into suitable portions and brush both sides with some oil. Place in a buttered casserole. Slice tomatoes and let them simmer in butter together with chopped onion for about 15 minutes. Add water and pour this sauce over fish. Sprinkle breadcrumbs on top and bake in pre-heated oven (Regulo 7—450° F.) for about 30 minutes. Sprinkle with chopped parsley and serve with mashed potatoes.

SMOKED COD OR HADDOCK

Norwegian

4 SERVINGS

2 lb. smoked cod or haddock fillets
4 oz. butter

Place fillets in a fish kettle with boiling water and allow to poach gently for 10—15 minutes. Melt butter and pour into sauce bowl. Drain fish and place on hot serving dish. Boiled potatoes and boiled carrots or spinach, moistened with butter, are usually served with this.

HADDOCK BAKED WITH SPINACH

Norwegian

4 SERVINGS

1½ lb. haddock fillets
8 oz. chopped frozen spinach
1 oz. butter
1 tablespoon flour

top of the milk
3 tablespoons breadcrumbs
salt and pepper

Wash and dry haddock fillets. Place in a buttered casserole. Season with salt and pepper. Melt butter in a saucepan and stir in flour. Add top of the milk (about 3 tablespoons) and stir in spinach. Season to taste with salt and pepper. Spread spinach over fish and sprinkle breadcrumbs on top. Bake in pre-heated oven (Regulo 7—450° F.) for about 30 minutes. Serve with mashed potatoes.

HADDOCK BAKED IN WHITE SAUCE

Norwegian

4 SERVINGS

1½ lb. haddock fillets
1 oz. butter
¾ pint milk

2 tablespoons flour
3 tablespoons grated cheese
salt, pepper and lemon juice

Wash and dry fillets. Butter a casserole and put in fillets. Season with salt, pepper and lemon juice. Melt butter in a saucepan and stir in flour. Add milk gradually while stirring, and let sauce simmer for a few minutes. Season to taste with salt and pepper. Pour this sauce over fish and sprinkle grated cheese on top. Bake in pre-heated oven (Regulo 7—450° F.) for about 35 minutes. Serve with boiled potatoes.

HADDOCK AND CELERIAC

Norwegian

4 SERVINGS

1½ lb. haddock fillet
1 celeriac (or 1 cup diced celery)
1 tablespoon chopped onion
1 oz. butter

2 tablespoons flour
3 tablespoons chopped parsley
salt and pepper
paprika and lemon juice

Peel and dice celeriac. Place in a saucepan and add enough water to just cover it. Wash and dry haddock and place in a bowl that fits on top of saucepan. Cover tightly and let it all cook. The fish and celeriac should both be done in the same time. Melt butter in another saucepan and stir in flour. Add water from celeriac together with stock collected from fish, stirring constantly until sauce is smooth. Add onion and season with salt, pepper, lemon juice and paprika to taste. Let it simmer for a few minutes. Separate fish into flakes and add to celeriac, mixing gently. Pour sauce over it and let it come to the boil again. Sprinkle with chopped parsley before serving with boiled potatoes.

SMOKED HADDOCK WITH SPINACH

Norwegian

4 SERVINGS

1½ lb. smoked haddock
12 oz. frozen chopped spinach
4 oz. butter

2 tablespoons flour
6 tablespoons top of the milk
1 hard-boiled egg

De-frost spinach. Let haddock boil in water for about 10 minutes. In the meantime, melt 1 oz. of butter in saucepan and stir in flour. Add milk gradually while stirring and then stir in spinach. Let it simmer on a very low flame for 5 minutes. Drain haddock and remove all skin and bones. Place in centre of hot serving dish. Put spinach in a ring around fish. Melt rest of butter and add chopped hard-boiled egg to it. Pour into a sauce bowl and serve with fish. Mashed potatoes go well with this.

HADDOCK BAKED IN TOMATO SAUCE (I)

Norwegian

4 SERVINGS

1½ lb. haddock fillets
½ tablespoon salt
½ tablespoon vinegar
2 tablespoons chopped dill

3 tablespoons tomato purée
1 tablespoon flour
¼ pint water

Wash and dry fillets. Mix salt and vinegar together and rub over fillets. Butter a casserole and place fish in it. Mix tomato purée with flour and dill and then stir in the water. Pour this sauce over fish. Cover casserole and bake in pre-heated oven (Regulo 7—450° F.) for about 30 minutes. Serve with boiled potatoes.

HADDOCK BAKED IN TOMATO SAUCE (II)

Norwegian

4 SERVINGS

1½ lb. haddock fillets
3 tablespoons chopped onion
2 tablespoons tomato purée
3 tablespoons chopped parsley
3 tablespoons oil

3 tablespoons dry white wine
(or lemon juice)
2 oz. butter
3 tablespoons breadcrumbs
salt and pepper

Wash and dry haddock fillets. Place in a buttered casserole and season with salt and pepper. Mix chopped onion and parsley and sprinkle over fish. Mix oil, tomato purée and wine and pour on top. Sprinkle breadcrumbs over this and dot with butter. Bake in pre-heated oven (Regulo 7—450° F.) for about 30 minutes. Serve with mashed potatoes and green salad.

HADDOCK IN CHEESE SAUCE

Swedish

4—6 SERVINGS

2 lb. fillet of haddock
1 pint water
1 slice onion
2 oz. butter
2 tablespoons flour

¼ pint top of the milk
2 tablespoons grated
  Parmesan cheese
4 oz. peeled shrimps
breadcrumbs
salt and pepper

Soak fish in cold, salted water (3 tablespoons salt to 2 pints water) for 15 minutes. Remove fish and discard water. Bring 1 pint water to the boil in a fish kettle. Add slice of onion and salt lightly. Place fish fillets on grating, lower gently into water and allow to simmer for about 10 minutes. Wipe a suitable casserole with buttered paper and place fish fillets in it. Reduce fish stock to ¾ pint. Melt 1 oz. butter in saucepan and stir in flour. Add stock very gradually, stirring all the time and letting sauce thicken before more stock is added. Add milk, season with salt and pepper to taste. Allow to simmer for 10 minutes. Pour over fish. Sprinkle cheese and a few breadcrumbs on top. Melt rest of butter and also sprinkle on top. Place under grill so that cheese melts and surface is slightly browned. Garnish with shrimps and serve with mashed potatoes.

BOILED PIKE

Swedish

4 SERVINGS

1 pike (about 2½ lb.)   boiled potatoes
1 tablespoon salt for   melted butter
  each pint water   fresh grated horseradish

Clean fish, scrape off scales and trim off fins. Soak in salted water (1½ tablespoons to 1½ pints water). Remove fish and discard water. Heat water and salt and place pike in it on its underside just before water boils. There should be enough water to just cover fish. Bring to the boil and skim off any foam. Allow to simmer for 20 minutes, when meat should be loosened from the bone. Test gently with fork. Serve fish whole with boiled potatoes, melted butter and freshly grated horseradish.

HALIBUT ON BACON AND VEGETABLE BED

Swedish

4 SERVINGS

2 lb. sliced halibut   2 tablespoons sliced celery
4 slices bacon   1 teaspoon chopped dill
8 oz. carrots   2 teaspoons salt
1 large onion   4 slices lemon
4 oz. mushrooms   2 oz. butter
2 tablespoons chopped parsley pepper
½ pint dry white wine

Wash carrots, scrape if necessary and slice rather thinly. Place bacon slices in shallow casserole. Spread carrots over. Chop onion and mushrooms and spread over carrots.

Sprinkle with parsley, celery, dill, 1 teaspoon salt and a little pepper. Place fish slices on this bed and sprinkle with rest of salt. Place lemon slices on top, dot with butter and pour wine over. Cover tightly with foil and bake in heated oven (Regulo 5—400° F.) for 20 minutes. Remove foil and bake for another 20 minutes. Serve with mashed potatoes and green salad.

ROLLED FISH FILLETS

Swedish

4 SERVINGS

1½ lb. fillet of sole or plaice
anchovy fillets

1 oz. butter
breadcrumbs

Soak fish fillets for 5—10 minutes in cold, salted water (3 tablespoons salt to 2 pints water). Remove fillets and dry well on a clean cloth. Discard water. On each fish fillet place one anchovy fillet and roll it tightly towards the tail. Secure with a toothpick. Butter shallow oven dish and place rolls closely together in it. Sprinkle breakcrumbs on top and place butter in dots on top of that. Bake in pre-heated oven (Regulo 7—450° F.) for 15—20 minutes. Serve with boiled new, potatoes, buttered and sprinkled with chopped parsley.

BUTTER POACHED FISH FILLETS

Swedish

4—6 SERVINGS

2 lb. fish fillet to taste   salt and pepper
3 oz. butter

Soak fish in cold salted water (3 tablespoons salt to 2 pints water) for 10 minutes. Remove fish and dry it well. Melt butter in shallow oven dish and place lightly seasoned fillets in it. Cover fish with buttered paper and cook for 10 minutes in pre-heated oven (Regulo 7—450° F.). If fillets are thick, turn over after 5 minutes. Serve with fish sauce to taste (see page 68) and boiled or mashed potatoes.

BAKED EEL

Swedish

4 SERVINGS

1 eel (2 lb.)   1 egg
1½ teaspoons salt   3 tablespoons breadcrumbs
juice of ½ lemon   2 oz. butter

Have fishmonger skin and fillet eel. Rub with salt and lemon juice. Beat egg and brush over eel. Roll in breadcrumbs and place in buttered baking dish. Dot with butter and bake in heated oven (Regulo 6—425° F.) for 30—40 minutes, basting from time to time. Serve either hot or cold, with baked potatoes and strong fish sauce (see page 72).

BOILED SALMON

Swedish

4 SERVINGS

4 salmon steaks	7 white peppercorns
2 pints water	1 slice onion
4 tablespoons vinegar	¼ carrot
1 tablespoon salt	fresh dill
½ teaspoon sugar	1 lemon for garnish

Soak salmon for 10 minutes in cold salted water (3 tablespoons salt to 2 pints water). Discard water. Put all the spices in water and allow to boil in covered fish kettle for 10 minutes. Place salmon steaks on the grating and lower into boiling water. Bring to the boil again and skim off any foam. There should be just enough water to cover fish. Simmer without a cover for about 15 minutes.

Salmon can be served hot, garnished with sliced lemon, hollandaise sauce and boiled new potatoes.

If it is to be served cold, liquid should be strained over it before it is set to cool, to prevent it from getting too dry. Best served with mayonnaise mixed with 1 carton sour cream and fresh chopped dill.

LUNCHEON MACKEREL

Swedish

4 SERVINGS

4 mackerel	4 teaspoons freshly
2 tablespoons vinegar	grated horseradish
8 tablespoons mayonnaise	salt and pepper

Clean and fillet mackerel. Wash fillets and place in sauce-pan. Pour in just enough water to cover and add vinegar, salt and pepper. Bring to the boil and allow to simmer for 10—15 minutes, or until mackerel is done. Cool in own stock overnight. Place mackerel fillets on serving dish. Mix mayonnaise and horseradish and spread on each fillet. Serve with boiled new potatoes and green salad.

JANSON'S TEMPTATION

Swedish

4 SERVINGS

10 tinned Swedish anchovies, or	4 oz. butter
4 fillets of pickled herring	2 cartons single cream
5 medium potatoes	(each 2·7 fluid oz.)
2 medium onions	

Clean and fillet anchovies. If herring is used, cut each fillet into strips. Cut onion into slices and sauté in some of the butter until transparent. Peel potatoes and slice fairly thinly. Butter a casserole and place half the sliced potatoes in it. Spread onions on top and then anchovies or herring, finishing with the rest of the potatoes. Dot remainder of butter on top and place in pre-heated oven (Regulo 5—400° F.) for about 10 minutes. Then pour half the cream over it and replace in oven, letting it cook for another 10 minutes. Add rest of cream and continue cooking until potatoes are done, about 1 hour in all. Serve immediately with green salad.

FISH TURBANS

Swedish

4 SERVINGS

1 lb. fillet of sole or plaice	¼ pint fish stock
1 tin crab meat (5 oz.)	1 tin evaporated milk
8 oz. mushrooms	(equivalent to ¾ pint diluted)
3 oz. butter	2 tablespoons grated
1½ tablespoons flour	Parmesan cheese
breadcrumbs	salt
paprika	

Served in small individual oven dishes.

Soak fish fillets for 5—10 minutes in cold, salted water (3 tablespoons salt to 2 pints water). Remove, dry carefully on a clean cloth and discard water. Slice mushrooms (do not wash or peel them as this destroys some of the flavour) and fry lightly in 2 oz. of butter. Chop crabmeat and add to mushrooms. Save liquid to make up part of fish stock, which is made from boiling a few fish scraps. Sprinkle flour on top of mushrooms and crabmeat, and stir in. Add fish stock and tinned milk gradually, stirring gently until sauce has thickened. Season to taste. Wipe oven dishes with buttered paper. Stand a fish fillet on its side, inside edge of each dish, so that it forms a circle. Divide sauce mixture between each dish, placing it in the middle. Bake in pre-heated oven (Regulo 5—400° F.) for about 10 minutes. Sprinkle cheese, breadcrumbs and a dash of paprika on top of each one. Distribute remainder of butter on top of this. Place under grill until they turn golden and cheese is melted. Serve with boiled or mashed potatoes and green salad.

STEWED SHRIMPS AND EGGS

Swedish

4—6 SERVINGS

6 hard-boiled eggs	¾ pint milk
10 oz. shrimps	2 tablespoons chopped dill
1½ oz. butter	salt and pepper
3 tablespoons flour	

Peel hard-boiled eggs and keep warm by placing in warm water. Melt butter in saucepan and stir in flour. Add milk gradually while stirring, until smooth. Simmer for at least 5 minutes. Season to taste with salt and pepper. Mix in shrimps and dill. Pour on to heated dish. Cut eggs in halves and place in a ring around dish. Serve with toast.

FISH SOUFFLÉ

Swedish

4 SERVINGS

2 cups boiled fish	4 eggs
2 oz. butter	2 tablespoons breadcrumbs
3 tablespoons flour	salt and pepper
¾ pint milk	

Melt butter in saucepan and stir in flour. Add milk gradually, stirring until smooth and creamy. Remove from heat. Beat egg yolks and add to sauce, beating vigorously. Divide fish into small flakes and add to sauce. Season to taste with salt and pepper and allow to cool. Beat egg whites until very stiff and fold into sauce. Butter soufflé tin and pour mixture in. Sprinkle with breadcrumbs and bake in heated oven (Regulo 3—325° F.) for 1 hour or until set. Serve immediately with mushroom, shrimp or fine fish sauce, see pages 70 and 72.

SMOKED BUCKLING WITH EGGS

Swedish

4 SERVINGS

4 smoked buckling	3 tablespoons flour
2 hard-boiled eggs	¾ pint milk
2 tablespoons chopped	salt and pepper
chives (or parsley)	
1½ oz. butter	

Remove all skin and bones from fish and divide into pieces. Peel and chop eggs. Melt butter in a saucepan and stir in flour. Add milk gradually while stirring, until smooth. Simmer for at least 5 minutes. Season with salt and pepper. Stir in smoked fish, eggs and chives (or parsley). Bring to the boil again and serve with fried potatoes.

CREAMED LOBSTER

Swedish

4 SERVINGS

1 tin lobster (5 oz.)	1 small tin evaporated milk
2 oz. butter	(equivalent to ¾ pint diluted)
2 tablespoons flour	salt and cayenne pepper
water	

Drain lobster and save liquid. Divide into suitable pieces. Add to the liquid 1 tin evaporated milk and enough water to make up ¾ pint in all. Melt butter in saucepan and stir in flour. Add liquid gradually, stirring until sauce is smooth and creamy. Simmer for 5 minutes. Add lobster and season to taste with salt and a little cayenne pepper. Re-heat, but do not boil as this makes lobster tough. Serve as filling for plain omelette or in pastry cases.

LOBSTER SALAD

Swedish

4 SERVINGS

1 tin lobster (5 oz.)
1 small tin baby peas (14 oz.)
1 small tin asparagus tips
   (10 oz.)
1 stalk celery

1 carton double cream
   (2·7 fluid oz.)
mayonnaise
lettuce
salt and pepper

Clean and scrape celery. Cut it across in thin slices. Drain vegetables well and place in a bowl together with celery. Cut lobster into slices and add as well. Beat cream until it is thick when mixed with mayonnaise (half the quantity suggested on page 73). Then pour it over the salad and mix gently, using 2 forks. Season to taste. Chill for 30 minutes. Place the washed and well-drained lettuce leaves on a serving dish and pile salad on top.

LOBSTER SOUFFLÉ

Swedish

4 SERVINGS

1 tin lobster or crab (5 oz.)
4 eggs
3 oz. butter
3 tablespoons flour

1 small tin evaporated milk
   (equivalent $\frac{3}{4}$ pint diluted)
1 tablespoon dry Vermouth
salt and cayenne pepper

Drain lobster and cut up into small pieces, saving liquid. Separate egg whites and yolks, beating yolks a little. Dilute tinned milk with water to make $\frac{1}{2}$ pint in all, add lobster juice. Melt butter in saucepan and stir in flour. Gradually add liquid, stirring vigorously until sauce is thick and smooth.

Reduce heat and stir in egg yolks. Stir vigorously whilst heating for about 3 minutes, when sauce should have consistancy of mayonnaise. Do not let it boil. Remove from heat and stir in lobster, Vermouth, salt and cayenne pepper to taste. Allow to cool. Beat egg whites very stiff and carefully fold into lobster mixture. Pour into unbuttered soufflé mould and bake in heated oven (Regulo 3—350° F.) for about 1 hour, when it should be set and golden. Serve immediately with melted butter to which a little lemon juice is added, or with fine fish sauce (see page 69).

SPRAT CASSEROLE (I)

Swedish

4 SERVINGS

1½ lb. sprats
2 tablespoons strong prepared mustard
1 carton double cream (2·7 fluid oz.)
chopped chives

2 tablespoons butter
breadcrumbs
salt

Clean sprats, open and remove bone, keeping them in one piece. Trim off fins, wash carefully and drain well. Prepare casserole by wiping with buttered paper and coating with breadcrumbs. Beat cream until thick and stir in mustard. Salt each sprat lightly and spread some cream and mustard mixture on the inside. Roll them up separately with skin on outside. Place side by side in casserole. Sprinkle chopped chives over them and dot with butter. Cover with thin layer of breadcrumbs. Place in heated oven (Regulo 5—400° F.) for about 30 minutes, when it should be golden brown. Serve with fried potatoes and green salad.

SPRAT CASSEROLE (II)

Swedish

4 SERVINGS

1½ lb. sprats	2 tablespoons butter
4 medium cold, boiled potatoes	3 tablespoons tomato purée
2 teaspoons French mustard	1 carton single cream
1 tin anchovy fillets	(2·7 fluid oz.)
	breadcrumbs

Clean and open sprats, remove bones carefully, keeping in one piece. Trim off fins, wash and drain well. Prepare casserole by wiping with buttered paper and coating with breadcrumbs. Dice potatoes and place in bottom of casserole. Spread mustard on top. Cut anchovy fillets so that there is one piece for each sprat. Roll sprat around it tightly, skin side out, and pack into casserole. Dot butter on top and cover with thin layer of breadcrumbs. Place in heated oven (Regulo 5—400° F.) for 10 minutes. Remove casserole and pour cream mixed with tomato purée over it. Replace in oven for another 10—15 minutes, when most of the cream should have been absorbed. Serve with green salad.

BAKED WHITING WITH CHEESE SAUCE

Norwegian

4 SERVINGS

2 lb. whiting	1 carton single cream
4—5 oz. cream cheese spread	(2·7 fluid oz.)
1½ teaspoons paprika	2 tablespoons lemon juice
1 tablespoon chopped chives	salt

Fillet and wash the whiting. Dry fillets and place in a buttered casserole. Season with salt and lemon juice. Bake in pre-heated oven (Regulo 7—450° F.) for 10 minutes. In the meantime, put cheese in bowl and stir with fork. Add paprika and chopped chives. Continue stirring while adding cream, a tablespoon at a time. Keep stirring until all cream is added and sauce is soft and smooth. When fish is ready, sauce is spread over it. Serve with baked potatoes and green salad.

FISH BALLS

Swedish

4 SERVINGS

1 lb. fillet of cod or haddock	1 carton single cream
4 oz. butter	(2·7 fluid oz.)
1½ tablespoons flour	1 carton double cream
2 eggs	(2·7 fluid oz.)
salt and pepper	1 pint fish stock

Soak fish fillets for 10—15 minutes in cold, salted water (3 tablespoons salt to 2 pints water). Remove and drain fish, discarding water. Place fillets with skin down on a wooden board and scrape fish until all meat is minced. Place meat in bowl and pound together with butter. Pass it through a sieve to get smooth, even texture. Season lightly with salt and pepper. Beat egg yolks, flour and single cream together. Add cream mixture to fish, a little at a time, while stirring vigorously. Then add double cream in same manner. Beat egg whites stiff and stir in carefully. Bring fish stock to the boil. Use teaspoons to form the mixture into round balls. Dip spoons in hot stock to prevent sticking. As fish balls are formed, place in boiling stock. Allow to boil for about 10 minutes. Make a sauce from the stock (see shrimp sauce, page 72). Shrimps can be omitted for this dish as the sauce is quite good on its own. Pour sauce over fish balls and serve with boiled potatoes and vegetable to choice.

FISH FILLETS WITH MUSHROOMS AND VEGETABLES

Swedish

4—6 SERVINGS

2 lb. fish fillets
  (plaice, sole, halibut)
¾ pint fish stock
4 oz. mushrooms
3 tablespoons leek, sliced
6 tablespoons carrots
  (cut in small cubes)
3½ oz. butter

1½ tablespoons flour
1 small tin evaporated milk
  (equivalent to ¾ pint diluted)
2 egg yolks
2 tablespoons top of milk
2 firm tomatoes
salt and pepper

Soak fish in cold, salted water (3 tablespoons salt to 2 pints water) for 10 minutes. Make fish stock from fish scraps, and strain. Slice mushrooms and fry in 2½ oz. butter, together with leek and carrots. Season with a little salt and pepper, add 3 tablespoons of fish stock, cover and allow to simmer until vegetables are soft. Remove fish from cold water and poach in fish stock for 5—10 minutes. Melt remainder of butter in a saucepan and stir in flour. Add ½ pint of fish stock gradually while stirring, letting sauce thicken each time before more stock is added. Stir in evaporated milk, season to taste, and allow to simmer for a few minutes. Mix egg yolks and cream together and add to sauce while stirring vigorously. Add vegetable mixture to sauce. Place fish fillets on hot serving dish and pour sauce on top. Garnish with quartered tomatoes and serve with boiled potatoes.

MEAT AND POULTRY

Swedish meatballs are no doubt the best-known Scandinavian main course. They are both economical and easy to make, and a popular family dish. Children in particular seem to love it. Many of the other recipes also have special appeal because of the seasoning and rich gravies which are typically Scandinavian. Try braised spring chicken with its parsley stuffing or boiled lamb in dill sauce, for example, both subtly different in flavour from the way these meats are usually prepared outside Scandinavia.

BEEF STEAK WITH ONIONS

Swedish

4 SERVINGS

2 lb. sirloin steak $\frac{1}{4}$ pint water
3 oz. butter   salt and pepper
4 medium onions

Cut steak into 4 slices and pound flat. Sprinkle with salt and pepper. Peel and slice onions and fry them until nicely brown in half the butter. Remove onions and keep warm. Add rest of butter and fry meat on high flame, about 4 minutes on each side. Place steaks on hot serving dish. Pour water into frying pan whilst still on the flame and stir so that meat juices blend with it. Pour over steaks and garnish with fried onions. Serve immediately with potatoes to choice and green salad.

ROLLED BEEF WITH ANCHOVY STUFFING

Swedish

4 SERVINGS

$1\frac{1}{2}$ lb. skirt of beef   1 tablespoon flour
8 anchovy fillets $\frac{1}{2}$ pint water
2 tablespoons chopped parsley   1 bouillon cube
3 tablespoons chopped onion   salt and pepper
2 oz. butter

Cut meat in to 4 equal portions and pound flat. Season with pepper and very little salt. Chop anchovy finely and mix with parsley and onion. Divide mixture equally and spread on meat. Roll each piece and secure with toothpicks. Warm a cast iron pot and brown the rolled meat in half the butter, taking care all sides are evenly browned. Sprinkle with flour, pepper and pinch of salt. Melt bouillon cube in water and pour on meat. Cover tightly and cook slowly for 1½ hours, basting from time to time. Remove toothpicks and serve in its own sauce with fried potatoes and a boiled vegetable.

MINCED BEEF A LA LINDSTROM

Swedish

4 SERVINGS

1½ lb. minced beef (lean)
2 egg yolks
4 oz. cold boiled potatoes
4 oz. boiled beetroots
2 tablespoons grated onion
2 tablespoons vinegar

3 oz. butter
sliced beetroot for garnish
parsley
salt and pepper
2 tablespoons chopped capers

Slice beetroots and let them marinate in the vinegar for 20 minutes. Remove from vinegar and chop finely. Mince potatoes or chop very finely. Place meat in bowl and mix in egg yolks. Season lightly with salt and pepper. Work mixture until it is smooth, using a wooden spoon. Stir in potatoes, beetroots, grated onion and capers. Taste and season again if necessary. Form into 12 cakes, about ¾ inch thick. Brown 1 oz. butter in a large frying pan, preferably of cast iron, and place 4 meat cakes in it, frying them quickly on both sides on a high flame. Keep warm whilst remainder are fried in the same manner. Place on a warm serving dish and pour browned butter over. Garnish with parsley and sliced beetroot. Serve immediately with fried potatoes.

BRAISED BEEF ROLLS WITH BACON

Swedish

4—6 SERVINGS

2 lb. skirt of beef	2 oz. butter
8 slices bacon	1 bouillon cube
4 frankfurters	$\frac{1}{4}$ pint water
2 teaspoons mustard	3 tablespoons top of the milk
2 tablespoons flour	salt and pepper

Pound meat thin and flat. Cut into 8 strips about 4 inches by $2\frac{1}{2}$ inches and sprinkle both sides with salt and pepper. Spread one side with mustard and place a strip of bacon and $\frac{1}{2}$ frankfurter on each slice. Roll up and secure with toothpicks. Roll in flour and fry in butter, using a cast iron frying pan, until nicely browned on all sides. Bring water to boil in saucepan and dissolve bouillon cube. Pour over meat, cover and simmer until tender, about 1 hour. Remove beef rolls to a casserole, take out toothpicks and keep warm. Add cream to frying pan whilst stirring, simmer for few minutes and pour over meat. Serve with fried potatoes and vegetable to choice.

SWEDISH POTROAST

6 SERVINGS

3 lb. silverside or chuck steak	*Sauce:* 2 tablespoons fat
suet	$2\frac{1}{2}$ tablespoons flour
1 oz. butter	1 small tin evaporated milk
1 small carrot	$\frac{3}{4}$ pint stock
1 medium onion	parsley
$\frac{3}{4}$ pint water	gherkins
1 bouillon cube	
salt and pepper	

Clean meat with damp cloth and cover with suet. Heat a large cast iron pot and brown butter. Brown meat on all sides, turning it gently with 2 wooden spoons. Cut onion and carrot in quarters and brown together with meat. Dissolve bouillon cube in water using a small saucepan. When meat is brown, remove from flame and pour some of the stock at the side of it. Cover with tight-fitting lid and place in heated oven (Regulo 3—350° F.) cooking for about 2 hours. Keep adding rest of stock, basting meat occasionally. When roast is tender, remove from pot, keeping it warm whilst sauce is prepared. Strain stock into saucepan and skim off 2 tablespoons of fat. Heat this in cast iron pot and work in flour to a smooth paste. Add warm stock slowly, stirring vigorously to prevent lumps forming, or burning. Simmer for a few minutes while stirring in tinned milk. Season with salt and pepper to taste. Slice meat across the grain, place on warm serving dish garnished with parsley and sliced gherkins, serve with sauce and boiled or mashed potatoes.

KIDNEY AND MUSHROOM SAUTÉ

Swedish

4 SERVINGS

1½ lb. calves' kidneys	¼ pint white wine
8 oz. mushrooms	1 small tin evaporated milk
3 oz. butter	(equivalent to ¾ pint diluted)
1 tablespoon flour	1 tablespoon grated onion
½ pint stock	salt and pepper

Slice mushrooms and fry in 1 oz. butter. Remove all fat from kidneys and slice evenly. Fry gently in rest of butter for a few minutes. Season with salt and pepper, add mushrooms and sprinkle flour on top. Stir and slowly add stock, wine and evaporated milk. Cover tightly and simmer for 15 minutes. Stir in onion, season to taste and serve very hot.

BOILED BEEF WITH HORSERADISH SAUCE

Swedish

6 SERVINGS

3 lb. rib of beef	1 oz. butter
1 large carrot	2 tablespoons flour
1 small parsnip	1 pint stock
½ celeriac	3 tablespoons grated fresh
(or ½ cup diced celery)	horseradish
1 large onion	salt and pepper
water	

Rinse meat and place in just enough boiling water to cover. Bring to the boil and skim off any foam. Peel vegetables and add them whole, together with salt and pepper. Boil gently for about 3 hours, skimming again if necessary. To make the sauce, melt butter in a small saucepan. Add flour, stirring continuously until smooth. Stir in hot stock from meat and boil for a few minutes. Season with salt and pepper to taste. Add grated horseradish. The sauce must not boil after the horseradish is added, as it may then become bitter. Slice meat and place on a serving dish, garnished with vegetables. Serve with boiled potatoes.

BEEF STROGANOFF À LA SUÉDOISE

Swedish

4 SERVINGS

1½ lb. skirt of beef	2 tablespoons dry sherry
2 oz. butter	1 small tin evaporated milk
1 large onion	salt and pepper
2 tablespoons tomato purée	

Cut meat into even strips, about 1 inch thick. Chop onion finely and soften in a little of the butter, using a cast iron frying pan. Remove onion and brown strips of meat in remaining butter. Season with salt and pepper. Lower the flame and stir in onion, tomato purée and evaporated milk. Cover the pan and simmer for 30 minutes. Add the sherry, season to taste and simmer for another 10 minutes. Serve with boiled macaroni.

STEWED STEAK

Swedish

4 SERVINGS

2 lb. stewing steak	3 large onions
2 teaspoons salt	15 black peppercorns
¼ teaspoon white pepper	3 bay leaves
3 tablespoons flour	1 pint water
2 oz. butter	½ tablespoon soya sauce

Cut meat into suitable pieces and peel and slice onions. Mix flour, salt and pepper on a plate and turn pieces of meat in it until coated with flour. Brown onions in butter, using cast iron pot. Add meat, peppercorns and bay leaves and allow to brown on all sides, turning gently with 2 wooden spoons. Bring water and soya sauce to the boil in a separate pot, then pour over meat. Cover tightly and simmer for about 3 hours, stirring occasionally. Serve with boiled potatoes and Swedish cranberries.

SAILOR'S BEEF

Swedish

4 SERVINGS

2 lb. skirt of beef	¾ pint water
2 oz. butter	1 bouillon cube
3 large onions	2 lb. peeled potatoes
2 teaspoons salt	2 bay leaves
¼ teaspoon white pepper	

Cut meat into fairly large pieces and pound them flat. Peel and slice onions. Cut potatoes into ½-inch thick slices. Brown onions in a little of the butter. Remove them and brown meat in rest of the butter. Season with salt and pepper and remove from pan. Warm water in same pan, melting bouillon cube in it. Place potatoes, meat and onions in a casserole in as many layers as necessary, but making top and bottom layers of potatoes. Place bay leaves at the sides and pour bouillon over it. Cover tightly and cook in heated oven (Regulo 5—400° F.) for about 1½ hours. Serve with green vegetable.

BEEF STEW

Danish

6 SERVINGS

2½ lb. stewing beef	2 bay leaves
3 lb. potatoes	2 tablespoons dripping
3 large onions	salt and pepper
1 pint water	butter
1 bouillon cube	

Melt dripping in large cast iron pot. Peel, slice and brown onions in dripping. Cut meat into 1-inch cubes and add to pot. Peel and cut potatoes and add. Put in bay leaves, salt and pepper. Dissolve bouillon cube in boiling water and add to pot. Cover tightly and simmer for about 3 hours. Stir all ingredients well, as they should disintegrate, as in a hash. Serve in soup plates with a dot of butter topping each helping.

VEAL CUTLET OSCAR

Swedish

4 SERVINGS

4 slices veal fillet or
cutlet (boneless)
2 oz. butter
1 tin asparagus spears
(10—14 oz.)

1 tin lobster (2—4 oz.)
salt and pepper
fine steak sauce
(see page 74)

Pound the veal flat and sprinkle with salt and pepper. Make sauce as directed and keep warm over hot water. Heat asparagus and lobster by placing tins in boiling water. Melt butter in frying pan and brown meat on both sides. Place meat on hot serving dish and put a few asparagus spears on top of each slice. Arrange rest of asparagus around meat and cover with some sauce. Top each portion with lobster meat and serve immediately, serving rest of sauce separately. Baked potatoes and green salad are the usual accompaniment to this delicious meal.

VEAL BIRDS

Swedish

4 SERVINGS

1½ lb. veal fillet
8 slices boiled ham
8 slices cheese
2 tablespoons oil

¼ pint boiling water
3 tablespoons top of the milk
3 tablespoons flour
salt and pepper

Have butcher cut meat into 8 slices and pound very thin.
Mix flour with a little salt and pepper and turn meat slices
in this. Place 1 slice ham and 1 slice cheese on each piece
of meat and fold up, securing with toothpicks. Heat oil in
cast iron frying pan and brown meat quickly on all sides.
Pour boiling water over meat, cover and simmer for about
30 minutes. Place meat in hot serving dish, remove toothpicks and keep warm. Add cream to stock while stirring
over low flame. Simmer for a few minutes, season to taste
and pour over meat. Serve with Southern Fried Potatoes
(see page 104) and vegetable to choice or green salad.

ROLLED VEAL WITH MUSHROOM STUFFING

Swedish

4 SERVINGS

1½ lb. boneless stewing veal
8 oz. mushrooms
3 oz. butter
½ pint water
1 bouillon cube

1 tablespoon flour
½ gill cream
1 small carrot
1 medium onion
salt and pepper

Cut meat into 4 equal portions and pound them flat. Season
with salt and pepper on one side. Slice mushrooms, leaving

peel on, and fry in 1 oz. butter. Season to taste. Place fried mushrooms on each slice of meat, roll up and secure with toothpicks. Brown together with carrot and onion in 1 oz. butter, using cast iron pot. Melt bouillon cube in water and pour over meat. Cover tightly and cook gently for 1 hour, basting occasionally. Remove toothpicks and place meat in a casserole, keeping it warm. Pour stock into a container, discarding carrot and onion. Brown remaining butter in cast iron pot, stir in flour to a smooth paste, add warm stock stirring continuously and simmer for a few minutes. Then add cream and bring to the boil again. Season to taste. Pour sauce over meat and serve with mashed potatoes and a vegetable.

ROAST LEG OF LAMB

Swedish

6 SERVINGS

4 lb. leg of lamb	1 tablespoon cream
2 teaspoons salt	2 tablespoons flour
¼ teaspoon pepper	½ pint milk
1 teaspoon sugar	1 teaspoon redcurrant jelly
½ pint made coffee	

Rub meat with salt and pepper, place in oven pan and roast in heated oven (Regulo 4—375° F.) for 1½ hours. Mix coffee with sugar and cream and pour over roast. Continue to roast, while basting from time to time, for another hour, when meat should be done. Remove on to serving dish and keep warm. Strain liquid from pan and skim off fat. Add milk to stock to make 1 pint in all. Put 2 tablespoons of fat back in pan and place on low flame. Stir in flour and add stock gradually while stirring until thick and smooth. Pour into sauce bowl and add redcurrant jelly. Serve with potatoes and vegetable to choice.

BOILED LAMB OR VEAL WITH DILL SAUCE

Swedish

6 SERVINGS

3 lb. shoulder of lamb, *or*
   3 lb. best neck end of veal
2 pints water
4 white peppercorns
fresh dill
¾ tablespoon salt
1 oz. butter

2 tablespoons flour
1 pint stock
2 tablespoons chopped dill
1½ tablespoons vinegar
1 egg yolk
1½ tablespoons sugar
1 tablespoon cold stock

Rinse meat and place in boiling water, which should be just enough to cover it. Bring to the boil and skim off any foam. Add peppercorns, salt and a few sprigs of dill. Boil gently for about 2 hours, skimming again if necessary. To make sauce, melt butter in a small saucepan. Add flour, stirring continuously until smooth. Stir in 1 pint hot stock and boil for a few minutes. Add chopped dill, vinegar and sugar. Mix egg yolk and cold stock together and add to the sauce, stirring vigorously until it comes to the boil again, when it is ready. Slice meat and place in a casserole, pour sauce over and garnish with a few sprigs of dill. Serve with boiled potatoes.

FRICASSÉE OF LAMB OR VEAL

Swedish

6 SERVINGS

3 lb. shoulder of lamb, *or*
   3 lb. best neck end of veal
2 pints water
4 white peppercorns
1 bay leaf
1 clove
1 medium onion
¾ tablespoon salt

1 oz. butter
2 tablespoons flour
1 pint stock
1 teaspoon lemon juice
½ teaspoon sugar
1 egg yolk
2 tablespoons cream
lemon and parsley for garnish

Rinse meat and place in just enough boiling water to cover. Bring to the boil and skim off any foam. Stick clove in onion and add this together with peppercorns, bay leaf and salt. Boil gently for about 2 hours, skimming again if necessary. To make sauce, melt butter in a small saucepan. Add flour, stirring continuously until smooth. Stir in 1 pint of hot stock and boil for a few minutes. Add lemon juice and sugar. Mix cream and egg yolk together and add to sauce, stirring vigorously until it comes to the boil again. Slice the meat and place on a serving dish, garnished with lemon slices and parsley. Serve with boiled rice.

FINE LAMB STEW

Swedish

4 SERVINGS

2 lb. shoulder lamb, boned
3 tablespoons flour
1 tablespoon salt
¼ teaspoon pepper
1 tablespoon meat dripping
3 cloves garlic
¾ pint water
2 bouillon cubes

4 tablespoons tomato paste
2 bay leaves
2 stalks sliced celery
1 lb. small onions
8 oz. new carrots
1 lb. new potatoes
2 tablespoons chopped
  parsley

Cut meat into 1-inch cubes and turn in mixture of flour, salt and pepper. Melt dripping in large cast iron pot, add meat and brown on all sides. Dissolve bouillon cubes in boiling water and add to pot together with chopped garlic, tomato paste, bay leaves and celery. Bring to the boil, cover and simmer for 30 minutes. Clean and slice carrots. Peel onions and if very small leave whole. Peel potatoes and add these vegetables to pot, stirring to mix with meat and stock. Cover and continue to simmer for another 40 minutes, when meat and vegetables should be tender. Sprinkle with parsley and serve.

LAMB AND CABBAGE

Swedish

6 SERVINGS

3 lb. stewing lamb
3 lb. white cabbage
3 teaspoons salt
10 white peppercorns

2 bay leaves
parsley
1 pint water

Cut meat into suitable pieces. Cut cabbage into 8 pieces.

Place meat and cabbage in layers in a cast iron pot, adding salt, peppercorns and bay leaves evenly distributed. Pour water over, cover tightly and bring to the boil. Skim off any foam, reduce heat and simmer for about 2 hours. Sprinkle with chopped parsley and serve with boiled potatoes.

If a stronger flavour is desired, meat and cabbage should be browned in butter before water is added.

One can also cook potatoes together with meat and cabbage, when a little more water will be needed. It is then best not to add cabbage and potatoes until meat has boiled for 1 hour.

FINNISH LAMB STEW

4 SERVINGS

2½ lb. stewing lamb	1 tablespoon salt
2 lb. peeled potatoes	¼ teaspoon pepper
8 oz. carrots	1 tablespoon chopped parsley
2 leeks	1½ pints water

Cut meat into suitable pieces and slice potatoes, carrots and leeks. Place meat and vegetables in as many layers as necessary in a casserole, seasoning between the layers. Pour water over it, cover tightly and cook in heated oven (Regulo 3—350° F.) for about 2½ hours. Sprinkle chopped parsley on top and serve.

ROAST PORK WITH PRUNES

Swedish

6 SERVINGS

3 lb. loin of pork	½ pint water
½ lemon	salt and pepper
15 prunes	

Clean meat with damp cloth. Make 3 lengthwise cuts in meat, the middle one somewhat deeper. After rinsing prunes well in lukewarm water, halve them and remove stones. Stuff cuts in meat with halved prunes and tie securely. Rub joint carefully with lemon, brown on all sides in a cast iron pot, adding a little butter if necessary. Season with salt and pepper. Place meat with fattest side up, pour heated water at side of meat, cover with tight fitting lid and place in heated oven (Regulo 3—350° F.). Baste occasionally, if necessary adding a little water. After about 2 hours roast should be tender. Remove from pot, slice and serve with strained stock and mashed potatoes. Meat can be garnished with additional boiled prunes if so desired.

SAVOURY PORK CHOPS

Swedish

6 SERVINGS

6 lean pork chops	2 tablespoons flour
½ pint water	1½ tablespoons paprika
1 bouillon cube	2 tablespoons catsup
8 oz. mushrooms	¼ pint cream
4 slices bacon	salt and pepper
2 chopped onions	little fat for frying

Sprinkle chops with salt and pepper and fry until golden

brown on both sides, using just enough fat to avoid sticking. Place pork chops in shallow oven dish. Pour water into frying pan and dissolve bouillon cube in it whilst stirring. Pour into bowl and keep. Slice mushrooms and place over chops. Cut bacon into fairly small pieces and fry slowly together with chopped onion for about 10 minutes. Sprinkle with paprika and flour. Add cream and bouillon gradually, stirring until smooth. Simmer for 5 minutes. Stir in catsup and season to taste with additional salt and pepper, as sauce should be rich and spicy. Pour over chops and mushrooms and bake in heated oven (Regulo 4—375° F.) for about 30 minutes. Serve with boiled rice and green salad.

POTROAST OF PORK

Swedish

6 SERVINGS

3 lb. leg of pork	1 teaspoon marjoram
2 tablespoons margarine	1 tablespoon salt
¾ pint water	4 onions
1½ tablespoons vinegar	4 carrots
2 tablespoons tomato paste	2 tablespoons flour
2 bay leaves	garlic and pepper

Have meat cut into thick slices. Melt margarine in frying pan and brown slices well on both sides. Place in large cast iron pot. Rinse out frying pan with a little water and pour over meat. Mix rest of water with vinegar and tomato paste and pour over meat. Add spices, cover and simmer for about 1½ hours. Cut carrots into strips and peel and slice onions. Add vegetables to pot and simmer for another 30 minutes. Mix flour in a little cold water and stir in to thicken gravy. Simmer for a few minutes, season to taste and serve with boiled potatoes.

STUFFED PORK ROLLS

Swedish

4 SERVINGS

1½ lb. neck end of pork, boned   1 bouillon cube
1 apple   1 tablespoon flour
4 prunes   ½ gill cream
1 oz. butter   salt and pepper
½ pint water   ¼ teaspoon ground ginger

Cut meat into 4 equal portions and pound them flat. Sprinkle with ginger, salt and pepper. Peel, core and quarter the apple. Rinse prunes carefully in lukewarm water, halve them and remove stones. Place 1 piece apple and 1 prune on each slice of meat, roll up and secure with toothpicks. Brown in butter, using cast iron pot. Sprinkle with a little salt and pepper. Melt bouillon cube in water and pour over meat. Cover tightly and cook gently 45 minutes, basting occasionally. Remove toothpicks and place meat in casserole, keeping it warm. Stir flour into a little cold water, add boiling stock and stir vigorously to prevent lumps forming. When sauce is smooth and thick add cream and simmer for a minute or so. Pour sauce over meat and serve with fried potatoes.

PORK AND CABBAGE

Danish

6 SERVINGS

2½ lb. slightly salted pork   6 peppercorns
1 medium white cabbage

Remove outer leaves of cabbage, slice thinly and rinse in cold water. Place a layer of cabbage in large cast iron pot.

Cut up pork and place on top. Place rest of cabbage over pork. Add peppercorns and cover tightly. Simmer on very low flame for about 3 hours, when cabbage should be brown and meat tender. Serve with mashed potatoes.

ROLLED PORK WITH RED CABBAGE

Swedish

4 SERVINGS

1½ lb. neck end of pork, boned	1 lb. red cabbage
1 apple	1 large onion
1½ teaspoons salt	¼ pint water
4 prunes	4 cloves
¼ teaspoon pepper	3 tablespoons black-
2 oz. margarine	currant juice

Pour some boiling water over prunes and stand for few hours to soften. Remove from water, cut in half and take out pips. Peel, core and quarter apple. Cut meat into 4 equal slices and pound each one flat. Sprinkle with salt and pepper. Place ¼ apple and 1 prune on each slice, roll up and secure with toothpick. Brown in margarine. Cut cabbage into small dice and brown in remaining fat. Slice and brown onion. (If pork is very lean, some more margarine may be needed.) Mix onion and cabbage in cast iron pot. Place pork rolls on top. Add cloves and blackcurrant juice. Cover tightly and simmer for 45 minutes. Serve with boiled or mashed potatoes.

ROASTED SPARERIBS

Swedish

6 SERVINGS

4 lb. spareribs	½ teaspoon pepper
1 tablespoon salt	20 prunes
½ teaspoon ginger	1 bouillon cube
4 tart apples	¾ pint water

Have bones in spareribs cracked. Rub with mixture of salt, ginger and pepper. Place spareribs on grill in oven pan and bake in heated oven (Regulo 4—375° F.) for 45 minutes. Remove spareribs and pour off fat. Peel, core and slice apples. Wash prunes in warm water, halve, and remove pips. Spread apples and prunes in bottom of oven pan and place spareribs on top with inner side up. Dissolve bouillon cube in water and pour over meat. Replace in oven and bake for another 30 minutes. Turn ribs and put heat up to Regulo 5—400° F. Bake for another 20 minutes, when spareribs should be nicely brown. Remove meat, cut into portions and place on hot serving dish. Drain fruit and arrange around meat. Strain dripping into sauce bowl and serve with red cabbage (see page 113).

FRIED PORK

Swedish

4 SERVINGS

1½ lb. slightly salted or fresh, side pork

Cut pork into ¾-inch thick slices. Make 3 cuts across the rind on each slice. Heat a cast iron frying pan and add pork slices, frying them until crisp and brown on each side. If fresh pork is used, sprinkle with a little salt. Serve with onion sauce II (see page 80) and baked potatoes, or with brown beans (see page 106).

CHRISTMAS HAM

Swedish

ABOUT 20 SERVINGS

1 lightly salted ham (10—12 lb.)	1 egg white
2 bay leaves	1 tablespoon dry mustard
$\frac{1}{2}$ teaspoon peppercorns	1 tablespoon sugar
1 chopped onion	breadcrumbs
$\frac{1}{2}$ teaspoon allspice	cooked prunes for garnish
1 chopped carrot	apple sauce for garnish

Place ham in large saucepan, fat side up, and cover with cold water. Bring to the boil and skim off any foam. Add bay leaves, peppercorns, allspice, onion and carrot. Cover and simmer gently for 2 hours. Turn ham over and simmer for another 2 hours, when ham should be cooked through. Remove from stock. Skin ham and remove loose fat. Return to stock and leave overnight to cool. Remove ham from stock and wipe dry. Mix egg white, mustard and sugar. Brush this over ham so that it covers all fat. Sprinkle generously with breadcrumbs, place in large oven pan, fat side up, and bake in heated oven (Regulo 3—350° F.) for about 50 minutes, when it should be golden brown. Serve either cold on smorgasbord, or hot with red cabbage (see page 113) and potatoes to choice.

MINCED BEEF WITH ONIONS

Swedish

4 SERVINGS

1½ lb. minced beef   5 tablespoons water
2 large onions   salt and pepper
3 oz. butter

Peel, slice and fry onions in half the butter. Remove from frying pan, but keep warm. Form minced meat into cakes, about ½ inch thick and 2½ inches in diameter. Sprinkle with a little salt and pepper on each side. Brown rest of butter and fry meat over fairly high heat, about a minute on each side. Add water and spread onions on top. Cover the pan and simmer for 5 minutes. Serve directly from pan or arrange on hot serving dish, pouring over the sauce from the pan. Mashed potatoes are very good with this.

MEAT LOAF

Danish

4 SERVINGS

8 oz. minced veal   1 pint boiled milk
8 oz. minced pork   1 grated onion
1 egg   breadcrumbs
3 tablespoons flour   salt and pepper

Butter a suitable mould and sprinkle with breadcrumbs. Place meat and egg in bowl and mix well. Work in flour and add milk very gradually, stirring until it is all absorbed. Mix in grated onion and season to taste with salt and pepper. Put mixture into prepared mould and bake in bain marie in heated oven (Regulo 5—400° F.) for about 1 hour. Turn out on to warm serving dish, decorate with mixed boiled vegetables and serve with boiled macaroni and melted butter.

STUFFED CABBAGE

Swedish

4 SERVINGS

1 medium white cabbage	1 pint water
2 oz. rice	1 bouillon cube
1 lb. minced beef	2 tablespoons flour
1 egg	1 small tin evaporated milk
1 gill milk	salt and pepper
2 oz. butter	

Core and boil cabbage, using a teaspoon of salt to each pint of water, until it has softened and the leaves are starting to come away. Rinse rice in cold water and boil until fairly soft, drain and cool. Place meat in bowl and mix in egg, milk and rice. Use wooden spoon and work mixture until smooth, seasoning with salt and pepper to taste. Place a large spoonful of filling on each cabbage leaf, fold into small packages and tie each one together with fine string. Brown on all sides in butter, place in oven dish, rinse out frying pan with a little water and pour it over. Cover tightly and cook in heated oven (Regulo 5—400° F.) for about 1 hour. Heat water and melt bouillon cube. Mix flour with evaporated milk. Pour juice from stuffed cabbage into a saucepan, and stir in milk and flour. Put on a low flame, stirring continuously. When it starts to thicken, stock should be added gradually. Season to taste and simmer for 10 minutes. Serve the sauce separately. Boiled potatoes are usually eaten with this dish.

MEAT LOAF IN TOMATO SAUCE

Swedish

4 SERVINGS

1 lb. minced beef
1 large chopped onion
3 large slices white bread
1 egg

¼ pint water
1 leek
1 tin tomato soup
salt and pepper

Remove edges from bread. Beat egg and water lightly and crumble bread into it. Add chopped onion, meat and 4 tablespoons tomato soup. Mix together thoroughly. Season to taste with salt and pepper. Form into loaf and place in buttered oven pan. Clean leek and slice across thinly. Sprinkle over meat and pour on rest of tomato soup. Bake in heated oven (Regulo 6—425° F.) for 45 minutes. Serve with mashed potatoes.

SWEDISH MEATBALLS

4 SERVINGS

1½ lb. minced beef
1 egg
1 large onion
3 slices white bread
¼ pint water
3 oz. butter

2 tablespoons flour
1 pint water
1 tin evaporated milk
(equivalent to ¾ pint diluted)
½ teaspoon soya sauce
salt and pepper

Mix egg and ¼ pint water in a bowl. Crumble bread into it, letting it soak until thoroughly broken up. Remove any hard edges. Chop onion finely and fry lightly in a little butter. Add to mixture together with minced beef. Mix all thoroughly, using wooden spoon, until it is smooth and holds together. Moisten a wooden board with cold water. Form mince into round balls, about 1 inch in diameter, and place on the board. Brown rest of butter and fry meatballs evenly on all sides, placing them in a saucepan as they are finished. Stir flour into butter left in frying pan, working to a smooth paste. Heat water and add gradually, stirring all the time. Let it come to the boil and thicken before more is added. Stir in tinned milk and soya sauce. Pour sauce over meatballs and simmer together for about 15 minutes. Season to taste and serve with mashed or boiled potatoes and Swedish cranberries.

MEATBALLS IN CELERIAC SAUCE

Danish

5 SERVINGS

8 oz. minced veal	1 large celeriac or 1 cup celery
8 oz. minced pork	¾ pint water
1 egg	2 tablespoons flour
3 tablespoons flour	2 oz. butter
1 pint boiled milk	puff pastries for garnish
1 grated onion	salt and pepper

Make mince mixture as in Meat Loaf (see page 198). Form mince into meatballs about 1 inch in diameter. Put water to boil with a little salt and add meatballs. Allow to boil for about 5 minutes, then remove from water. Peel and dice celeriac and put to boil in same water until tender, about 15 minutes. Remove celeriac from water. Melt butter in saucepan and stir in flour. Add stock gradually while stirring until sauce is thick and smooth. Put meatballs and celeriac into sauce and bring to the boil. Season to taste and serve garnished with small puff pastries.

BOILED BEEF TONGUE

Swedish

6 SERVINGS

1 fresh beef tongue (about 3 lb.)	5 cloves
4 pints water	2 bay leaves
2 tablespoons salt	1 sliced carrot
1 teaspoon black peppercorns	1 sliced onion

Boil water in large pot and put in tongue. Bring to boil again and skim off any foam. Add all other ingredients and simmer for 2½ hours. Set to cool in stock. After 1 hour remove tongue, skin it, and trim end. Replace in stock and keep until ready to serve either hot or cold. If served hot, heat tongue in stock. Drain just before serving, either cold on smorgasbord or hot with mushroom sauce (see page 76).

STEWED PIG'S HEART

Danish

5 SERVINGS

2 lb. pig's hearts	2 tablespoons flour
5 oz. butter	½ pint cream
4 tablespoons chopped parsley	salt and pepper

Open pig's hearts, remove sinews and vessels, wash well. Mix 4 oz. butter with parsley, divide between the hearts and stuff into their centre cavity. Sew hearts up. Season flour with salt and pepper. Turn hearts in this, so that they are well coated. Melt rest of butter in cast iron pot and allow to darken. Add hearts and brown well on all sides. Heat cream and pour over meat. Cover tightly and simmer for 2 hours. Season to taste with salt and pepper and serve with boiled potatoes.

POTROASTED VEAL

Swedish

6—8 SERVINGS

4½—5 lb. leg of veal	½ teaspoon allspice, whole
2 oz. butter	2 tablespoons flour
1 bouillon cube	1 small tin evaporated milk
¼ pint boiling water	(equivalent to ¾ pint diluted)
2 sliced carrots	salt and pepper
2 sliced onions	gherkins for garnish

Rub meat with salt and pepper. Melt butter in large cast iron pot and brown meat on all sides. Dissolve bouillon cube in boiling water and pour over meat. Add carrots, onions and allspice, cover and simmer gently for 1½—2 hours, when meat should be tender. Remove meat from stock and keep warm. Strain stock and return to pot. There should be about ¾ pint stock but, if not, add water to make up quantity. Mix flour in 3 tablespoons cold water and add stock gradually, while on low flame. Stir until smooth, then add evaporated milk and simmer whilst stirring until sauce is smooth and thick. Season to taste. Serve sauce from separate bowl. Slice meat and place on hot serving dish, garnished with sliced gherkins.

STUFFED VEAL FILLET

Swedish

4 SERVINGS

4 slices veal fillet
3 oz. butter
3 tablespoons chopped parsley

1 carton single cream
(2.7 fluid oz.)
salt and pepper

Pound veal fillets flat and season with salt and pepper. Mix
2 oz. butter with parsley and divide into 4 portions. Put
1 portion on each fillet and roll up. Secure with toothpicks.
Brown in rest of butter. Add a little water to pan and cover
it, letting veal simmer for 15 minutes. Place meat in a warm
casserole, remove toothpicks and keep warm. Add cream to
frying pan, stir and bring to boil. Pour sauce over meat and
serve with boiled rice or mashed potatoes.

VEAL CHOPS WITH MUSHROOMS

Swedish

4 SERVINGS

4 veal chops
2 tablespoons lemon juice
1 egg
4 oz. mushrooms
3 tablespoons oil
3 tablespoons chopped parsley

3 tablespoons breadcrumbs
1 small tin evaporated milk
(equivalent to $\frac{3}{4}$ pint
diluted)
water
salt and pepper

Sprinkle meat with salt, pepper and lemon juice on both
sides. Beat egg and brush over meat, coating both sides.
Chop 4 mushrooms finely and mix with parsley and breadcrumbs. Turn chops in this mixture. Heat oil in cast iron
frying pan and fry chops slowly until golden brown on both

sides, and cooked through. Place chops on hot serving dish and keep warm. Chop rest of mushrooms and fry lightly in same pan. Dilute evaporated milk to make $\frac{1}{2}$ pint in all and add to pan. Simmer until it thickens, season to taste and pour over chops. Serve with baked or mashed potatoes and string beans au gratin (see page 109).

LIVER IN CREAM SAUCE

Swedish

6 SERVINGS

1½ lb. ox or pig's liver
  (in one piece)
1 pint milk
1 small tin evaporated milk
  (equivalent to ¾ pint diluted)

3 oz. butter
2 tablespoons flour
½ teaspoon soya sauce
salt and pepper

Melt butter in a large frying pan and brown liver on all sides. Season with salt and pepper. Remove liver and place in cast iron pot. Pour milk over, cover and simmer for 45 minutes, taking care it does not burn. When liver is cooked, take out and slice very thinly. Re-heat frying pan containing browned butter. Stir in flour to smooth paste. Add hot milk from cast iron pot, stirring continuously and letting it simmer until it is evenly thick. Stir in evaporated milk and soya sauce. Season to taste. Strain sauce, as it tends to get lumpy from the milk. Put sliced liver back in cast iron pot, pour sauce over and simmer together for 5 minutes. Serve directly with boiled potatoes and Swedish cranberries.

LIVER STEW

Swedish

4 SERVINGS

1 lb. ox liver   2 oz. margarine
3 oz. bacon   ½ pint water
3 tablespoons flour   1 teaspoon paprika
2 medium onions   ¼ pint milk
1 teaspoon salt   pepper

Dice liver and bacon. Mix flour with salt and pepper. Turn liver and bacon in this mixture. Peel and chop onions. Melt margarine in frying pan and brown liver, bacon and onions. Stir in water and milk and bring to boil. Season with paprika, cover and simmer for 15 minutes. Serve with either boiled rice or mashed potatoes, which should be formed in a ring on hot serving dish. Pour liver stew in middle.

FRIED CALVES' LIVER WITH CREAM SAUCE

Swedish

4 SERVINGS

1 lb. calves' liver   ½ pint cream
2 tablespoons flour   salt and pepper
3 oz. butter

Have liver cut into 4 nice slices. Mix flour with some salt and pepper and turn liver slices in this. Heat butter in frying pan and fry liver for about 2 minutes on each side. Remove liver and add cream whilst stirring. Bring to boiling point and replace liver into pan. Cover and simmer gently for 5 minutes. Serve with mashed potatoes.

FRIED SWEETBREADS WITH MUSHROOMS AND BACON

Swedish

4 SERVINGS

2 lb. sweetbreads
2 pints water
1 tablespoon salt
1 tablespoon lemon juice
8 slices bacon

4 tablespoons breadcrumbs
12 oz. button mushrooms
4 oz. butter
salt and pepper

Soak sweetbreads for 1 hour in cold water, then drain well. Bring water to the boil and add salt and lemon juice. Add sweetbreads and simmer for 18 minutes. Remove sweetbreads and let stock cool. Replace sweetbreads in cold stock. Melt 1 oz. butter in saucepan. Cut mushrooms in half and sauté covered for 6 minutes. Season with salt and pepper and keep warm. Grill bacon slices until crisp and keep warm. Drain sweetbreads and cut into $\frac{3}{4}$-inch slices. Mix breadcrumbs with a little salt and pepper and turn sweetbreads in this. Melt rest of butter in frying pan until golden brown, add sweetbread slices and fry for 4 minutes on each side on fairly high flame, so that they become crisp and golden. Arrange sweetbreads in middle of large hot serving dish. Place bacon on one side and mushrooms on the other. Serve immediately with grilled tomatoes (see page 110), buttered toast and green salad.

ROAST GOOSE

Swedish

8—10 SERVINGS

1 12-lb. goose	½ teaspoon pepper
½ lemon	20 prunes
1½ tablespoons salt	2 teaspoons potato flour
6 cooking apples	

Wash and dry goose well. Rub outside with lemon. Rinse prunes carefully in lukewarm water. Boil them in water until soft. Drain and de-seed them. Wash, peel, core and slice apples. Put mixture of apples and prunes inside goose and sew up at both ends. Rub goose with salt and pepper. Place in oven pan and cover tightly with tin foil. Roast in heated oven (Regulo 5—400° F.) for about 2 hours. The exact time depends on age of goose. Remove tin foil and pour off stock which has collected. Replace goose in oven for 5—10 minutes to get crisp and brown. Mix flour in a little cold water and add to stock. If necessary add a little water to make desired quantity of sauce. Serve with roast potatoes and red cabbage.

BRAISED SPRING CHICKEN

Swedish

4 SERVINGS

2 spring chickens	¼ pint chicken stock
½ lemon	4 oz. butter
2 teaspoons salt	¼ pint double cream
¼ teaspoon pepper	4 tablespoons chopped parsley

Wash and dry chickens. Mix parsley with 2 oz. of butter. Put half of mixture in each chicken and tie up. Rub chickens with lemon all over outside. Sprinkle with salt and pepper and brown evenly in rest of butter. Place side by side in cast iron pot with breasts up. Rinse out frying pan with stock and pour over chickens. Add cream, cover and place in heated oven (Regulo 7—450° F.) for about 30 minutes. Baste from time to time. When they are ready, remove strings and cut chickens lengthwise in halves. Place on heated serving dish, garnished with parsley. Pour sauce into saucebowl and serve with roast potatoes and green salad.

BRAISED CHICKEN

Swedish

4 SERVINGS

1 small roasting chicken	6 tablespoons white wine
3 medium onions	$\frac{1}{4}$ pint chicken stock
8 oz. tinned tomatoes	1 lb. peeled potatoes
4 oz. mushrooms	salt and pepper

Make stock by boiling neck, heart, liver and gizzard of chicken. Remove fat from chicken and render down on slow heat. The chicken can be either whole or in pieces. Wash and dry carefully, season with salt and pepper and brown in some of chicken fat. Place in casserole. Clean and slice mushrooms and brown slowly. Slice onions and add to frying pan with mushrooms to brown lightly. Mix in tomatoes and arrange around chicken. Rinse out frying pan with stock and pour it over chicken. Cut potatoes fairly small and add as well. Pour over wine. Cover and bake in heated oven (Regulo 7—450° F.) for about 1 hour. Serve directly from casserole.

DEEP FRIED CHICKEN

Swedish

4 SERVINGS

4 pieces chicken for frying   ¼ pint lukewarm water
5 oz. self-raising flour   salt and pepper
2 tablespoons oil   oil for frying

Place flour in a bowl with a little salt and pepper. Stir in oil and water. Cover and stand for 2 hours. Wash and dry pieces of chicken. Heat oil. Dip chicken pieces in the batter and fry them for about 15 minutes. Drain well and serve with French fried potatoes and green salad.

FRICASSÉE CHICKEN

Swedish

4—6 SERVINGS

1 boiling fowl   ½ onion
2 pints water   1 carrot
¾ tablespoon salt   1 oz. butter
5 peppercorns   2 tablespoons flour
1 bay leaf   ¾ pint stock
1 clove   1 teaspoon lemon juice
2 sprigs parsley   ½ teaspoon sugar

Choose a suitably sized bird according to number of servings required and have it cut into pieces. Wash and dry pieces. Bring water to the boil and add chicken and spices. Bring to the boil again, skim off any foam, add vegetables and simmer until chicken is tender. The time depends on age of bird. Remove chicken and keep it warm. Strain stock and measure out ¾ pint to use for sauce. Melt butter in saucepan and stir in flour. Gradually add stock, stirring continuously until sauce is smooth and thick. Simmer for 10 minutes and season with lemon juice and sugar. Pour sauce over chicken and serve with rice.

ROAST VENISON

Swedish

8 SERVINGS

½ leg venison (3—4 lb.)
2 oz. fatty bacon
1 pint water
salt and pepper

1 small tin evaporated milk
(equivalent to ¾ pint diluted)
3 tablespoons flour

Wash meat carefully and dry in clean cloth. Place meat in oven pan and cover with strips of bacon. Brown meat for 30 minutes in fairly hot oven (Regulo 7—450° F.). Cover the pan carefully with tin foil. Let it roast in oven (Regulo 5—400° F.) for about 2 hours. When meat is tender, remove from pan, discard bacon and keep meat warm. Pour dripping into large cast iron frying pan and heat. Stir in the flour to a smooth paste, taking care to prevent burning or lumps forming. Rinse out oven pan with water, heat and gradually add to the frying pan. Let the sauce simmer for a few minutes. Stir in evaporated milk and season to taste. Colour should be light brown. Slice meat and place it in a large casserole. Pour sauce over, cover and simmer together for 5 minutes. Serve with boiled potatoes and Swedish cranberries.

MINCED VEAL CUTLET

Swedish

4 SERVINGS

13 oz. minced veal
3 oz. minced pork
3 cold boiled potatoes
1 egg
anchovy paste

½ pint milk
1 oz. butter
2½ oz. margarine
salt and pepper

Place potatoes in mixing bowl and mash them, using wooden spoon. Mix in veal and pork and stir in egg. Add milk gradually and stir in. Season to taste with salt and pepper. Form into cakes and fry slowly in margarine until nicely brown. Place on hot serving dish and pour fat from pan over. Mix butter with anchovy paste to taste. Form into little balls, placing one on each veal cutlet.

RABBIT IN CREAM SAUCE

Swedish

6 SERVINGS

6 large rabbit pieces
  (preferably leg
  and breast)
4 oz. butter
1 pint milk

1 small tin evaporated milk
  (equivalent to ¾ pint diluted)
1 teaspoon soya sauce
3 tablespoons flour
salt and pepper

Brown rabbit pieces in 2 oz. butter, using a large cast iron pot. Season with salt and pepper. Warm the milk and pour over. Cover and cook slowly for 1½ hours. Brown the rest of the butter slightly in a frying pan. Stir in flour to a smooth paste. Add milk from the rabbit, stirring constantly until texture is smooth and creamy. Add tinned milk and soya sauce. Season to taste with salt and pepper. Pour sauce over rabbit pieces, and simmer for 5 minutes. Serve with boiled potatoes and Swedish cranberries.

Very few desserts belong to one country only, and what is typically Scandinavian is sometimes only a slight variation on what is found in the recipes of other countries. There is perhaps less emphasis on pastries and puddings in Scandinavia, and more on fruit and fresh berries, particularly during the summer months when wild berries with cream are a favourite sweet. But there are a few desserts that must not be missed, and one is apple cake with vanilla sauce.

FRUIT SALAD

Swedish

6 SERVINGS

1 small tin apricots
2 cooking apples
2 pears
2 bananas

2 oranges
4 oz. green grapes
lemon juice and/or
    sugar to taste

Peel all the fresh fruit except grapes, remove seeds and dice into fairly small pieces. Place fruit in bowl. Pour syrup from apricots over it, dice apricots and add. Stir gently, add sugar and/or lemon to taste and chill for 30 minutes. Place in a serving dish and garnish with grapes (cut into halves and pitted). Serve plain or with whipped cream. For festive occasions, add a little Cointreau.

FRESH PLUM SALAD

Swedish

4 SERVINGS

2 lb. plums (several varieties)   lemon juice
4 oz. sugar to 1 pint water

Boil sugar and water until sugar is entirely melted. Add lemon juice to taste and let it cool. Pour into suitable serving bowl. Make a cut around the skin of each plum. Scald them in boiling water, peel, cut into halves and remove pips. Put into syrup. Press plums down into the syrup with a plate, so they are totally submerged. Stand in a cool place for 30 minutes or so, before serving.

FILLED ORANGE HALVES

Swedish

4 SERVINGS

4 oranges	a few grapes
1 banana	sugar
1 apple	double cream for garnish

Wash oranges, dry them and cut into halves. Scoop out orange pulp with a spoon, taking care not to break the skin. Peel apple and banana. Cut grapes in half and de-seed them. Dice rest of fruit fairly finely. Mix all fruit together with sugar to taste and stand 10 minutes in a cool place. Fill orange skins with the fruit salad. Garnish with whipped cream sweetened with a little sugar. Chill for 10 minutes and serve.

BANANA BOATS

Swedish

4 SERVINGS

4 bananas	a few grapes
1 orange	whipped cream for garnish
1 apple	sugar and lemon juice to taste

Wash and dry bananas carefully. Slice off one side of the skin, using a sharp knife. Scoop out pulp carefully so that peel remains whole. Peel apple and orange, remove seeds and dice them and the bananas rather finely. Wash grapes, cut into halves and remove pips. Mix all the fruit carefully in a bowl and add sugar and lemon juice to taste. Fill banana boats with this salad and garnish with whipped cream. Chill for about 30 minutes and serve.

STUFFED MELON

Swedish

6 SERVINGS

1 medium melon	sugar
8 oz. fresh berries	Curaçao

Wash and dry melon. Slice off the top and remove all seeds. Carefully scoop out the meat and cut into cubes. Mix melon cubes with fresh berries according to season. Put layers of fruit and sugar, dampened with Curaçao to taste, into melon shell. Decorate plate on which it is placed with spilled over berries. Serve chilled.

STRAWBERRY PARFAIT

Swedish

5 SERVINGS

1 lb. strawberries	2 egg yolks
3½ oz. sugar	2 teaspoons lemon juice
4 tablespoons water	½ pint double cream

Mix sugar and water in saucepan and simmer for 5 minutes. Place bowl in bain marie (or use double saucepan) and put in egg yolks. Beat yolks while gradually adding sugar mixture. Heat sufficiently to thicken mixture, but do not boil. Remove from water bath and continue to beat until cool. Clean strawberries and put some aside for garnish. Crush remaining strawberries and stir into mixture together with lemon juice. Beat cream until stiff and stir in. Pour into refrigerator tray and freeze until firm. Remove tray 5—10 minutes before serving, so that it softens a little. Cut up remaining strawberries. Turn parfait on to cold serving dish and cut into 5 thick slices. Garnish with cut up strawberries and serve.

RHUBARB CREAM

Swedish

4 SERVINGS

4 stalks rhubarb
½ pint water
grated peel of ½ lemon

5 oz. sugar
2 tablespoons cornflour

Clean rhubarb and cut into 1-inch pieces. Put water, sugar and lemon peel to boil. Add rhubarb and simmer until soft. Mix flour with a little cold water. Add this while stirring and simmer for 3 minutes. Pour into serving dish and set to cool. Sprinkle a little sugar and serve cold with whipped cream.

STEWED APPLES

Swedish

4 SERVINGS

2 lb. cooking apples
1 pint water

4 oz. sugar
lemon juice

Boil sugar and water until sugar is completely melted. Add lemon juice to taste. Peel apples, cut into halves and remove cores. Place apples in sugar syrup as they are ready. Simmer until just soft. Test with a sharp fork, but be careful not to break them. Pour into suitable serving dish and set to cool. Serve with plain cake.

Rhubarb, pears or mixed fruit can be stewed in the same manner.

RED PORRIDGE

Danish

4 SERVINGS

¾ pint blackcurrant juice   2½ tablespoons potato flour
sugar to taste   ¾ pint water

Put flour in a saucepan. Stir in juice gradually without heating. Add water and sugar to taste. Bring to the boil, stirring constantly. Remove from heat as soon as it has come to the boil and allow to cool for a few minutes, stirring occasionally. Place a warm serving bowl on a towel and pour porridge into it. Sprinkle a thin layer of sugar on top and let it set in a cool place. It is best prepared the day before it is to be eaten. Serve with thick cream and plain biscuits or cake.

RASPBERRY CREAM

Swedish

6—8 SERVINGS

1 lb. raspberries   4 tablespoons cornflour
7 oz. sugar   4 tablespoons water
1 pint water

Clean berries. Put 1 pint water to boil with sugar and simmer for 5 minutes. Add berries and continue to simmer for another 4 minutes. Mix cornflour with cold water and add to berries whilst stirring. Simmer for another 4 minutes. Pour into serving bowl and set to cool. Serve with milk or cream.

APPLE PURÉE

Swedish

4 SERVINGS

2 lb. cooking apples
water

brown sugar
lemon juice

Wash apples and remove stalks and any brown spots. Cut into 4 or 8 pieces, depending on size. Place in saucepan. Pour in just enough water to prevent them burning. Cover tightly and cook, stirring occasionally, until they fall apart. Place a fine sieve on a large bowl. Pass apples through, using a wooden spoon. Stir in brown sugar and lemon juice to taste, while the purée is still warm. Let it cool and serve with whipped cream.

SWEDISH APPLE CAKE

4—6 SERVINGS

2 lb. cooking apples
6 tablespoons demerara sugar
3½ oz. rusks

3 oz. butter
3 tablespoons
  ground almonds

Wash, peel and core apples. Cut into thin slices. Crush rusks into fine crumbs, using a rolling pin. Wipe large cake tin with buttered paper. Place layers of apples, sugar, rusks, pieces of butter and ground almonds in the tin. Save most of the butter to go on top of the last layer of crumbs. Bake in heated oven (Regulo 5—400° F.) for 50 minutes. Serve lukewarm with vanilla sauce (see page 82).

CREAM CAKE

Swedish

4 SERVINGS

3 eggs   ½ pint double cream
3 tablespoons sugar   ¼ teaspoon grated lemon peel
1½ tablespoons flour

Butter a cake tin generously. Beat egg yolks and sugar until
white and creamy. Beat egg whites until stiff. Whip cream.
Stir flour and lemon peel into egg yolks and sugar mixture.
Add whipped cream and egg whites and fold in carefully.
Pour into cake tin and bake in heated oven (Regulo 4—375° F.)
for about 45 minutes. A few minutes before it is ready,
sprinkle with a little sugar and replace in oven. Serve in its
tin immediately, with tinned strawberries.

STUFFED BAKED APPLES

Swedish

4 SERVINGS

8 medium cooking apples   2 tablespoons water
4 tablespoons ground almonds   1½ oz. melted butter
5 tablespoons sugar   4 tablespoons breadcrumbs

Mix 3 tablespoons sugar with almonds and water. Wash and
dry apples. Remove cores but leave apples whole. Puncture
skin all over apples with a fork. Stuff almond mixture in the
centre of apples, dividing equally between them. Coat with
melted, slightly cooled butter. Mix breadcrumbs with remainder of sugar and roll apples therein. Place in buttered
shallow oven dish. Bake in heated oven (Regulo 5—400° F.)
for about 1 hour or until they are soft. As the exact time

depends on their size, it is best to test them with a fork. Serve warm with whipped cream or vanilla sauce (see page 82).

SWEDISH PANCAKES

4 SERVINGS

2 eggs	3 oz. self-raising flour
½ teaspoon salt	½ oz. butter
2 tablespoons sugar	butter for frying
1 pint milk	

Beat eggs, milk, salt and sugar together. Place flour in a bowl and add milk mixture gradually, beating all the time to prevent lumps forming. Melt butter and add to the batter. Let it stand for 2 hours. Melt some butter in a frying pan and pour in enough batter to just cover the pan. Let it brown on one side and then turn it over to brown on the other. This is easier to do by cutting the pancake into 4 pieces and turning each individually. A medium flame is best, but it needs to be watched carefully to get the right golden colour. As it takes a while to fry all the pancakes, it is advisable to keep the finished ones warm in the oven, door open to prevent them drying. The pancakes should be placed in piles on a serving dish and served as soon as possible with Swedish cranberries. They are also good with strawberry jam or with sugar.

RICE PORRIDGE

Swedish

4 SERVINGS

6 oz. rice
1 oz. butter
¾ pint water
1½ pints milk

½ teaspoon salt
1½ tablespoons sugar
cinnamon

Rinse rice thoroughly. Melt ½ oz. butter in cast iron pot. Add ¾ pint water and bring to boil. Add rice and boil for 10—15 minutes or until water has boiled away. Add milk and simmer for another 45 minutes, stirring occasionally to prevent burning. Season with salt and sugar and stir in rest of the butter. Pour into serving dish and decorate with cinnamon, making it into a pattern of stripes or checks. Serve with milk and sugar.

POOR KNIGHTS

Swedish

4 SERVINGS

1 pint milk
12 slices white bread
1 egg
1½ tablespoons sugar

6 tablespoons flour
½ oz. butter
margarine for frying
½ teaspoon cinnamon

Place flour, cinnamon, salt and sugar in a bowl. Mix ½ pint milk and egg together. Add this gradually to the flour, stirring constantly until smooth. Melt butter and stir into mixture. Let batter stand for 2 hours. Trim off edges of bread slices and soak in ½ pint milk, being careful they do not break. Dip in batter and fry golden brown on each side in margarine. Serve with jam or sugar.

CRISP PANCAKES

Swedish

4 SERVINGS

3½ oz. flour
2 tablespoons sugar
½ pint water
3 oz. melted butter

½ pint double cream
butter for frying
jam

Place flour in bowl and gradually stir in water to a smooth batter. Allow to stand for 2 hours. Stir in sugar, cooled melted butter and whipped cream. Melt a little butter in frying pan and pour in sufficient batter to cover it thinly. Cook until golden brown on underside. Put a little jam in the middle and roll up the pancake. Place on hot serving dish and keep warm until all are done and ready to be served.

WAFFLES

Norwegian

4 SERVINGS

4 eggs
8 oz. flour
1 pint sour cream

2 tablespoons sugar
butter for the waffle iron

Beat eggs and sugar until light and creamy. Stir in a little flour and a little cream alternately until it is all mixed together. Bake in usual way, using a waffle iron. Sprinkle a little sugar on each waffle and serve immediately.

APPLE PANCAKE

Swedish

4 SERVINGS

pancake batter (see page 221)	1½ oz. butter
4 cooking apples	4 tablespoons sugar

Make pancake batter according to recipe on page 221. Wash, core and peel apples. Slice and fry slowly in butter until almost soft. Butter a large, shallow oven dish and place apple slices in it. Sprinkle with sugar and pour batter over. Bake in heated oven (Regulo 7—450° F.) for about 45 minutes, when pancake should be set and a golden brown. Divide into portions and serve with sugar.

LAYER PANCAKE

Swedish

6 SERVINGS

3 eggs	1 oz. butter
7 oz. self-raising flour	jam
1 teaspoon salt	¼ pint double cream
4 teaspoons sugar	5 almonds
1¾ pints milk	margarine for frying

Place flour, salt and sugar in a bowl. Add milk gradually while beating. Let batter stand for 1—2 hours. Beat eggs and stir in together with melted butter. Melt some margarine in a large frying pan and pour in enough batter to just cover the pan. Fry golden brown on both sides and place on a hot dish. Spread jam on pancake and continue in this way until all the batter is fried, and piled in layers with jam in between. Whip cream and decorate top with cream, jam, and strips of almonds. Serve immediately, slicing like a cake.

CHOCOLATE PUDDING

Swedish

4 SERVINGS

1¼ pints milk
5 tablespoons cornflour
5 tablespoons cocoa

6 tablespoons sugar
vanilla essence

Mix flour, cocoa and sugar in a saucepan. Stir in milk gradually until it is all mixed together. Bring to the boil while stirring vigorously, and simmer 3 minutes. Add vanilla essence to taste. Pour into serving dish and set to cool. To prevent skin forming a little sugar can be sprinkled over the top before cooling. Serve with milk or cream.

CHOCOLATE CHIFFON PUDDING

Swedish

6 SERVINGS

5 tablespoons cocoa
1 teaspoon instant coffee
3 tablespoons gelatine
3 tablespoons cold water
2 eggs

3½ oz. sugar
½ pint milk
1 teaspoon vanilla essence
½ pint double cream

Soften gelatine in cold water. Beat egg yolks and sugar until light and creamy. Stir in cocoa and milk. Pour into saucepan and bring to the boil whilst stirring. Add coffee, vanilla and gelatine and remove from fire. Cool until starting to set. Beat egg whites stiff and fold in. Whip cream and stir in, saving a little for garnish. Rinse mould in cold water and pour mixture into it. Chill until completely set. Turn out on to cold serving dish and garnish with rest of whipped cream. Nuts or almonds are also suitable garnish.

LEMON CHIFFON PUDDING

Swedish

6 SERVINGS

3 tablespoons lemon juice
2 teaspoons grated lemon rind
½ pint milk
3 eggs
5 oz. sugar

3 tablespoons gelatine
2 tablespoons cold water
¼ pint double cream
salt
¼ pint double cream for garnish

Heat milk in a double boiler, but do not let it boil. Beat egg yolks with half the sugar and a pinch of salt, add to milk whilst stirring. Keep stirring over simmering water until it begins to thicken. Mix gelatine in cold water and add to mixture, stirring until dissolved. Remove from water and cool. Stir in lemon rind and add lemon juice gradually. Chill in refrigerator for about 15 minutes, or until starting to set. Beat cream and fold in. Beat egg whites and remaining sugar until very stiff and fold in as well. Pour into individual serving dishes (first rinsed out with cold water) and chill until completely set. Garnish with whipped cream.

PINEAPPLE CHIFFON PUDDING

Swedish

6 SERVINGS

½ pint pineapple juice
2 tablespoons lemon juice
3½ oz. sugar
2 eggs

3 tablespoons gelatine
2 tablespoons cold water
½ pint double cream
1 small tin pineapple cubes

Beat egg yolks with half of sugar until light and creamy. Stir in fruit juices. Put water and gelatine in saucepan and heat whilst stirring until dissolved, but do not allow to boil. Pour into mixture and chill for about 30 minutes or until starting to set. Beat cream until stiff and fold in. Beat egg whites and remaining sugar until very stiff and fold in as well. Cut up half of pineapple pieces so that they are not too large and stir in. Rinse a mould with cold water and pour in mixture. Chill for at least 3 hours, or until completely set. Turn out on to serving dish, garnish with remaining pineapple pieces and serve.

CARAMEL CHIFFON PUDDING

Swedish

6—8 SERVINGS

6 tablespoons gelatine	1 teaspoon vanilla essence
5 tablespoons water	1½ teaspoons grated orange rind
4 eggs	3 tablespoons rum
5 tablespoons sugar	½ pint double cream
½ pint milk	

Soften gelatine in cold water. Beat egg yolks with 4 tablespoons sugar until light and creamy. Heat milk in double boiler and stir in egg and sugar. Allow to get sufficiently hot to thicken whilst stirring but do not boil. Stir in gelatine, vanilla, orange rind and rum. Remove from double boiler and cool, stirring occasionally until starting to set. Beat egg whites until stiff. Add remaining sugar and continue beating until sugar is dissolved. Fold into mixture. Beat cream and fold in as well as crushed caramel. Pour into mould brushed with oil and chill until set. Turn out on cold serving dish and garnish with caramel strips (see page 228).

CARAMEL STRIPS

Swedish

10½ oz. sugar   8 tablespoons chopped almonds
butter

Melt sugar in dry frying pan over low flame, whilst stirring.
Add chopped almonds, stirring until it bubbles and turns
golden. Pour on to well buttered metal sheet. Dip knife in
oil and mark out 6 strips. Cut strips with oiled scissors,
working very quickly before caramel hardens. Shape into
half circle by pressing around jar. Crush remaining caramel
and use for flavouring caramel pudding.

CARAMEL CUSTARD

Swedish

6 SERVINGS

5½ oz. sugar   2 tablespoons sugar
3 tablespoons boiling water   ¾ pint milk
4 eggs   sliced almonds
¼ teaspoon salt   ½ pint single cream
1 teaspoon vanilla essence

Melt sugar in dry frying pan over low heat whilst stirring.
Add boiling water and simmer until consistency is like syrup.
Pour into warm 8-inch cake tin, turning it so that all sides
are covered. Beat eggs with salt, vanilla and sugar until
light and creamy. Mix in milk and cream. Pour into cake tin
and bake in heated oven (Regulo 2—300° F.) placing tin in
oven pan. Pour hot water into oven pan until it stands ½ inch
below rim of cake tin. Bake until set, about 1 hour. Remove
from water at once and set to cool. Turn on to cold serving
dish. Sprinkle with sliced almonds and chill before serving.

ORANGE WHIP

Swedish

6 SERVINGS

4 eggs
7 oz. sugar
2 teaspoons grated orange
  rind
½ pint pure orange juice

¼ pint pure lemon juice
3 tablespoons gelatine
3 tablespoons water
¼ pint double cream for
  garnish

Beat egg yolks with half of sugar until light and fluffy. Stir in orange rind and fruit juices. Put water and gelatine in saucepan and heat whilst stirring until dissolved, but do not allow to boil. Stir into orange mixture and chill for about 30 minutes or until it begins to set. Beat egg whites and remaining sugar until very stiff and fold into mixture. Pour into individual serving dishes (first rinsed out with cold water) and chill until completely set. Garnish with whipped cream and serve.

BAKED APPLES

Swedish

4—6 SERVINGS

8 medium cooking apples   butter
5—7 tablespoons syrup

Wash and dry apples. Remove cores, but leave apples whole. Puncture the skin all over the apples, using a fork. Butter a suitable shallow oven dish, place apples in it and pour syrup over them. Bake in heated oven (Regulo 5—400° F.) for about 45 minutes. The exact time will depend on the size of the apples. Baste from time to time. Serve with cream and sugar.

APPLE AND ALMOND CAKE

Swedish

6—8 SERVINGS

1 oz. butter	7 oz. sugar
7 oz. ground almonds	2½ tablespoons flour
2 eggs	apple purée (see page 219)
1 egg yolk	breadcrumbs

Make apple purée as directed on page 219, using 1½ lb. apples. Place butter in a bowl and beat with wooden spoon until white and creamy. Beat eggs, egg yolk and sugar until white. Mix with butter, add almonds, then blend in flour. Butter suitable oven dish and sprinkle with breadcrumbs. Cover bottom and sides with part of the dough. Add apple purée and cover with rest of dough. Bake in heated oven (Regulo 3—350° F.) for about 1 hour. Allow to cool in its dish for ½ hour. Turn out and serve with whipped cream or vanilla sauce.

PLUM SURPRISE

Swedish

6 SERVINGS

1 round plain cake	1 carton double cream
1 tin golden plums	(2.7 fluid oz.)
3—4 tablespoons liqueur to taste	1 carton single cream (2.7 fluid oz.)

Place cake on suitable serving dish with a slight edge. Pour juice from plums over cake, and allow to soak in, basting from time to time. Arrange plums on top and pour liqueur over. Mix the 2 cartons of cream and whip until stiff. Dot cream on top and serve.

CAKES AND PASTRIES

The Scandinavians have always been great coffee drinkers and take it after their meals as typically as the British drink tea. In country homes you will nearly always find a pot of coffee brewing. It is served with cake, whenever refreshment is required. Afternoon coffee parties are also common, and it is then that the enthusiastic cook brings out and serves home made cakes. The greater the variety of cakes and pastries the better, and if you are invited to such a party you must taste each kind, if you do not want to offend your hostess!

In Scandinavia it is also customary to bake for birthdays and holidays. Preparing for Christmas, even for the modern housewife, includes spending several days baking elaborately designed biscuits in large batches, to last through the season.

Home baking need not be a tiresome undertaking, and the appreciaton received in return usually makes it well worth while. The recipes in this section have been selected for their relative simplicity as well as for being typically Scandinavian.

TIGER CAKE

Swedish

4 eggs	7 oz. self-raising flour
8 oz. sugar	2½ tablespoons cocoa
7 oz. butter	grated peel of ½ lemon
¼ pint milk	butter and breadcrumbs for cake form

Butter cake form and sprinkle it with breadcrumbs.

Melt butter and set it aside to cool. Beat all the yolks and white of one egg with sugar until white and fluffy. Stir in flour, milk and melted butter alternately, a little at a time, until well mixed. Beat 3 remaining egg whites until stiff and fold in carefully. Pour half mixture into bowl and mix in grated lemon peel. Mix cocoa with other half of batter. Pour both mixtures in alternate layers into cake form and bake in heated oven (Regulo 4—375° F.) for about 1 hour.

CHOCOLATE CAKE

Swedish

2½ oz. block chocolate	¼ pint milk
6 oz. sugar	6 oz. self-raising flour
2½ oz. butter	1 tablespoon vanilla essence
2 eggs	butter and breadcrumbs for cake form

Butter cake form and sprinkle it with breadcrumbs.

Break up chocolate and put in a small bowl over boiling water until melted. Place butter, sugar, egg yolks and vanilla essence in a bowl and beat until smooth and creamy. Mix in melted chocolate, milk and flour alternately, a little at a time, until well mixed. Beat egg whites until stiff. Fold carefully into mixture, pour into cake form and bake in heated oven (Regulo 4—375° F.) for about fifty minutes.

FAVOURITE CAKE

Swedish

7 oz. butter	7 tablespoons boiling water
8 oz. sugar	grated peel of 1 lemon
2 eggs	butter and breadcrumbs for
6 oz. self-raising flour	cake form

Butter cake form and sprinkle it with breadcrumbs.

Mix butter and sugar until smooth and creamy. Stir in eggs and grated lemon peel. Stir in flour and water alternately, a little at a time, until well mixed. Pour into cake form and bake in heated oven (Regulo 4—375° F.) for about 45 minutes.

CAKE FOR COFFEE PARTIES

Swedish

15 oz. flour	*Garnish:*	1 beaten egg
7 oz. butter		3 tablespoons coarse sugar
1½ oz. yeast		for decorating
2 tablespoons sugar		1 tablespoon cinnamon
½ teaspoon salt		15 chopped almonds
1 egg		icing sugar
½ pint single cream		water glaze
3 oz. raisins		

Mix yeast with a little sugar. Place two thirds flour in mixing bowl. Cut butter into flour. Stir in yeast, sugar, salt, cream and egg. Work in rest of flour and raisins. Butter an oven pan and flatten out dough to fit. Set aside for 30 minutes to rise. Brush with beaten egg and sprinkle with coarse sugar, cinnamon and chopped almonds. Bake in heated oven (Regulo 6—425° F.) until golden. Glaze with icing sugar and water. Cut into squares and serve very fresh.

QUICK CAKE

Swedish

2 eggs	¼ pint milk
7 oz. sugar	2 teaspoons vanilla essence
1½ oz. butter	butter and breadcrumbs for
6 oz. self-raising flour	cake form

Butter cake form and sprinkle with breadcrumbs.

Beat eggs and sugar until white and fluffy. Add vanilla essence. Melt butter. Mix in milk, flour and butter alternately, a little at a time, until all mixed together. Pour into cake form and bake in heated oven (Regulo 4—375° F.) for about 45 minutes.

This cake is excellent with a fruit or chocolate filling topped with whipped cream.

ALMOND CAKE

Swedish

5 oz. butter	3 bitter almonds
7 oz. sugar	5 oz. self-raising flour
3 eggs	butter and ground almonds
2 oz. almonds	for cake form

Butter cake form and sprinkle it with ground almonds. Scald almonds and remove peels. Grind or chop them very finely. Stir butter thoroughly until it is white, using a wooden spoon. Beat egg and sugar until white and fluffy. Mix in butter gradually. Then stir in almonds and finally flour. Pour mixture into form and bake in heated oven (Regulo 4—375° F.) for about 40 minutes. This cake can be served plain.

PARSON'S GINGER CAKE

Swedish

2 eggs
6½ oz. sugar
¼ pint sour cream
3 oz. butter
1½ teaspoons ground ginger

5 oz. self-raising flour
2 teaspoons cinnamon
1½ teaspoons ground cloves
breadcrumbs

Butter cake form and sprinkle with breadcrumbs. Melt butter and allow to cool. Beat eggs and sugar until white and fluffy. Stir in cream and butter. Add spices and flour, stirring until smooth. Pour into cake form and bake in heated oven (Regulo 4—375° F.) for about 45 minutes. Allow to cool in form before turning out.

SOFT GINGER CAKE

Swedish

3 oz. rolled oats
5 oz. self-raising flour
10 oz. sugar
½ pint milk

1 teaspoon ground cloves
1 teaspoon cinnamon
1 teaspoon ginger
1 teaspoon ground cardamoms

Butter cake form and sprinkle with a little flour. Mix oats, flour, spices and sugar. Add milk whilst stirring until smooth. Pour into cake form and bake in heated oven (Regulo 4—375° F.) for about 45 minutes. Cool before turning out.

DARK CAKE

Swedish

1 egg	½ teaspoon ground cloves
4½ oz. sugar	1 oz. butter
¼ pint milk	¼ teaspoon cinnamon
5 oz. self-raising flour	breadcrumbs
1 tablespoon cocoa	

Butter cake form and sprinkle with breadcrumbs. Melt butter and cool. Beat egg and sugar. Add seasoning and a little milk and flour alternately, until well mixed. Then stir in butter, pour into cake form and bake in heated oven (Regulo 3—350° F.) for about 1 hour. Set to cool before turning out.

SOFT BROWN CAKE

Swedish

2 eggs	¼ pint sour cream
12 oz. sugar	2 teaspoons cinnamon
6½ oz. self-raising flour	1 teaspoon ground
3 oz. butter	cardamoms
	breadcrumbs

Butter cake form and sprinkle with breadcrumbs. Melt butter and cool. Beat eggs and sugar until light and fluffy. Stir in seasoning and melted butter, add sour cream. Stir in flour a little at a time. Pour into cake form and bake in heated oven (Regulo 3—350° F.) for about 45 minutes. Let it cool in form before turning out.

SILVER CAKE

Swedish

7 egg whites	3½ oz. butter
9 oz. sugar	10 almonds
4 oz. self-raising flour	
1 tablespoon potato flour	

Butter cake tin and sprinkle with scalded, peeled and chopped almonds. Melt butter and set to cool. Beat egg whites stiff and mix in sugar and both flours. Stir in butter, blending well, then pour into cake form and bake in heated oven (Regulo 4—375° F.) until done. Test with a skewer in the middle, and if skewer is dry then cake is ready. Let it cool before turning out.

SOUTHERN APPLE CAKE

Swedish

2 eggs	5 oz. flour
6½ oz. butter	4 cooking apples
8 oz. sugar	breadcrumbs

Beat sugar and butter until white and creamy. Mix in eggs and then flour. Stir until smooth. Butter a cake tin and sprinkle with breadcrumbs. Add cake batter. Peel apples, remove cores and slice thinly. Press apple slices down in batter. Bake in heated oven (Regulo 5—400° F.) for about 50 minutes. Allow to cool before turning out.

OAT CAKE WITH APPLES

Swedish

3 oz. sugar	6 tablespoons self-raising flour
3 oz. butter	6 tablespoons milk
1 egg	3 apples
2 oz. rolled oats	sugar
cinnamon	breadcrumbs

Butter cake form and sprinkle with breadcrumbs. Beat sugar and butter until creamy. Add egg and mix in well. Add milk, oats and flour, a little at a time, until all mixed in. Pour into cake form. Peel and slice apples. Dip in mixture of sugar and cinnamon and place in rings on cake. Press them down a little. Sprinkle some sugar and cinnamon over top. Bake in heated oven (Regulo 3—350° F.) for about 40 minutes. Turn out when lukewarm and serve immediately.

CHOCOLATE SANDWICHES

Swedish

10 tablespoons rolled oats	5 oz. butter
6 oz. sugar	10 tablespoons self-raising flour
3 tablespoons cream	
3 tablespoons syrup	1 teaspoon vanilla essence

Filling: chocolate cream (see page 252)

Melt butter and mix all ingredients. Butter an oven sheet and place tablespoons of batter on it, giving each one plenty of room as they spread considerably. Bake in heated oven (Regulo 4—375° F.) until golden. Sandwich two together with chocolate cream between.

CHOCOLATE STICKS

Swedish

5½ oz. self-raising flour 3 teaspoons cocoa
1 egg yolk 1 egg white
3½ oz. butter 8 tablespoons rolled oats
5 oz. sugar

Beat egg yolk, sugar and butter until light and fluffy. Mix in cocoa and flour, leaving a little flour for rolling out. Shape dough into long rolls and cut into 2-inch pieces. Brush with egg white and roll in oats. Place on buttered baking sheet, bake in heated oven (Regulo 4—375° F.) for about 15 minutes.

CHOCOLATE TOPS

Swedish

3½ oz. butter 3 tablespoons rolled oats
3½ oz. sugar 3 tablespoons potato flour
1 egg 5 tablespoons self-raising flour
3 tablespoons cocoa

Beat sugar and butter until light and fluffy. Work in egg and oats. Then stir in cocoa and flour. Butter a baking sheet carefully and place spoonfuls of dough on it, making them pointed upwards. Bake in heated oven (Regulo 4—375° F.) for about 15 minutes.

CHOCOLATE CUBES

Swedish

3½ oz. butter
1 egg yolk
3½ oz. sugar
5 oz. self-raising flour
chopped almonds

1 tablespoon cocoa
1 teaspoon vanilla essence
1 egg white

Beat sugar and butter until light and creamy. Stir in yolk, flour, cocoa and vanilla essence and mix well. Place on floured baking tray and make into 2 thick rolls. Brush with egg white and roll in chopped almonds. Place on buttered baking sheet and bake in heated oven (Regulo 6—425° F.) for about 15 minutes. Slice immediately with very sharp knife and spread out to cool.

CHOCOLATE ROLLS

Swedish

2½ oz. butter
8 oz. sugar
1 egg

15 tablespoons rolled oats
2 tablespoons self-raising flour
1 teaspoon cocoa

Melt butter and pour over oats. Stir in flour, sugar, egg and cocoa until well mixed. Butter a baking sheet carefully and dust with flour. Place spoonfuls of batter on sheet, leaving plenty of space for spreading. Bake in heated oven (Regulo 6—425° F.) until golden. Allow to cool a little before loosening with spatula and bending around stick to make rolls.

ALMOND ROLLS

Swedish

3½ oz. ground almonds   3½ oz. butter
1 tablespoon plain flour   2 tablespoons single cream
3½ oz. sugar

Mix all ingredients in saucepan and simmer for a few minutes.
Butter a baking sheet carefully and sprinkle with flour. Place
spoonfuls of batter on sheet, leaving plenty of room for
spreading. Bake in heated oven (Regulo 6—425° F.) until
golden. Loosen from sheet with spatula and curl around
stick when lukewarm.

NUT SQUARES

Swedish

2½ oz. self-raising flour   2 tablespoons cocoa
5 oz. sugar   ½ teaspoon vanilla essence
2½ oz. butter   7 tablespoons nuts
1 egg

Beat butter, egg and sugar until light and creamy. Mix in
cocoa and vanilla essence and then flour, stirring until well
blended. Cover oven tray with buttered paper and spread
mixture over paper. Sprinkle coarsely chopped nuts on top.
Bake in heated oven (Regulo 4—375° F.) for about 45 minutes.
Cut into squares whilst still hot.

BASIC BISCUIT DOUGH

Swedish

16 oz. self-raising flour   5 oz. sugar
10 oz. butter   1 egg

Beat egg, butter and sugar until light and creamy. Work in flour. This dough makes Vanilla Biscuits, Chocolate Hearts and Nut Sticks.

NUT STICKS

Swedish

one-third basic biscuit   beaten egg
    dough   coarse sugar for decorating
1 oz. chopped nuts

Mix chopped nuts into dough. Place on floured baking board and roll into long sticks, about ¾ inch in diameter. Cut sticks into 2-inch lengths and brush with beaten egg. Roll in coarse sugar, place on buttered baking sheet and bake in heated oven (Regulo 5—400° F.) until light golden in colour.

VANILLA BISCUITS

Swedish

one-third basic biscuit dough   chopped almonds
1 teaspoon vanilla essence   sugar
1 beaten egg

Mix vanilla essence into dough. Place on floured baking board and roll out. Use biscuit shape and cut out. Brush with beaten egg and sprinkle with chopped almonds and sugar. Place on buttered baking sheet and bake in heated oven (Regulo 5—400° F.) until light golden in colour.

CHOCOLATE HEARTS

Swedish

one-third basic biscuit dough   chopped almonds
2 teaspoons cocoa   sugar
beaten egg

Mix cocoa into dough. Place on floured board and roll out.
Cut out with heart-shaped biscuit form. Brush with beaten
egg and sprinkle with chopped almonds and sugar. Place on
buttered baking sheet and bake in heated oven (Regulo
5—400° F.) until crisp.

OAT LEAVES

Swedish

$3\frac{1}{2}$ oz. rolled oats $3\frac{1}{2}$ oz. butter
2 tablespoons glucose $3\frac{1}{2}$ oz. sugar

Mix all ingredients in saucepan and simmer for a few minutes.
Butter a baking sheet carefully and place tablespoons of batter
on it, leaving plenty of space for spreading. Bake in heated
oven (Regulo 6—425° F.) until golden. Loosen from sheet
with spatula and bend over rolling pin whilst hot.

DEEP FRIED SAILOR RINGS

Swedish

10 oz. self-raising flour   4 tablespoons single cream
2 eggs   sugar for garnish
$4\frac{1}{2}$ oz. sugar

Beat eggs, sugar and cream until light. Stir in flour. Form
into rings and deep fry in oil until golden. Drain and turn
in sugar.

GINGER BISCUITS
Swedish

13 oz. sugar	1 teaspoon ground cloves
½ pint syrup	½ pint double cream
12 oz. butter	2 lb. plain flour
1 tablespoon ginger	1 tablespoon bicarbonate
1 teaspoon cinnamon	of soda

Stir sugar and syrup for 10 minutes. Melt butter and add together with spices. Stir until well mixed. Beat cream for a few minutes and stir in. Mix flour and bicarbonate and work in, saving a little flour for rolling out. Knead dough well and keep in cool place overnight. Roll out dough thinly and cut into interesting shapes, such as hearts, animals, people, etc. Place on buttered baking sheet and bake in heated oven (Regulo 4—375° F.) until nicely brown. These biscuits are sometimes decorated with icing sugar and water, and used for making designs, especially at Christmas.

RAISIN SLICES
Swedish

5 oz. butter	2 egg whites
5 oz. sugar	3 tablespoons sugar
3 eggs	6 tablespoons raisins
6 bitter almonds	2 tablespoons chopped
5 oz. self-raising flour	orange peel
	8 almonds

Cream butter and sugar until light and fluffy. Add eggs one by one whilst stirring. Scald bitter almonds, peel and grate. Stir into dough. Mix in flour. Butter an oven pan and spread dough in it. Bake in heated oven (Regulo 5—400° F.) for 5 minutes. Beat egg whites until very stiff. Add 3 tablespoons sugar gradually whilst continuing to beat. Spread over cake. Scald almonds, peel and chop coarsely. Sprinkle orange peel, almonds and raisins over egg white. Replace in oven and bake for another 5 minutes, or until the meringue takes on colour. Allow to cool, cut into squares and serve whilst fresh.

DEEP FRIED CHRISTMAS COOKIES
Swedish

4 eggs	1½ oz. butter
1½ oz. icing sugar	1 tablespoon cognac
6 oz. plain flour	grated peel of ½ lemon

Melt butter and allow to cool. Stir yolks, sugar and cognac until well mixed. Add lemon peel and melted butter. Then stir in flour and knead well. Keep in cool place overnight. Place dough on floured baking board and roll out until thin. Cut into 1-inch strips. Cut strips diagonally to make 4-inch lengths. Make 1-inch slit in centre of each piece. Thread one end through centre hole and pull out on underside, so that they are knotted. Deep fry in oil until golden, and drain. These cookies keep well if kept in tins, and are often served with stewed fruit.

LUCIA CATS
Swedish

½ pint milk	25 almonds
6 oz. butter	5 bitter almonds
6 oz. sugar	10 tablespoons raisings
1 egg	*Garnish:*
1 sachet saffron	1 beaten egg
(5 grains)	coarse sugar
2 oz. yeast	10 chopped almonds
2 lb. flour	

Warm milk and saffron. Stir yeast with a little sugar. Mix flour, yeast, milk and egg to smooth dough. Stir sugar and butter until light and creamy and work into dough. Allow to rise for 30 minutes. Scald and chop almonds finely and work into dough together with raisins. Place dough on floured baking board and shape into buns. Make cut on 2 opposite sides of each bun, elongate corners a little and curl outwards. Place on buttered baking sheet and allow to rise for 20 minutes. Brush with egg and sprinkle with sugar and chopped almonds. Bake in heated oven (Regulo 7—450° F.) until golden brown.

MOTHER'S DEEP FRIED BUNS

Swedish

7½ oz. self-raising flour	6 tablespoons top of the milk
2 tablespoons sugar	grated peel of ½ lemon
1½ oz. butter	sugar and cinnamon for garnish
1 egg	

Melt butter and allow to cool. Beat egg and milk and add grated lemon peel. Stir in butter, sugar and flour. Beat until well mixed. Put teaspoons of batter in hot oil and deep fry until golden. Drain and turn in mixture of sugar and cinnamon.

SHROVE TUESDAY BUNS

Swedish

5 tablespoons double cream	*Filling:* ¼ pint double cream
5 tablespoons water	2 tablespoons sugar
2½ oz. butter	2 tablespoons
1 egg	ground almonds
2 tablespoons sugar	icing sugar
1 oz. yeast	
1 teaspoon sugar	
1 lb. flour	

Place cream, water and butter in saucepan and warm, allowing butter to melt. Mix yeast with 1 teaspoon sugar. Beat egg and sugar until light and creamy. Work in liquid, yeast and flour to a smooth dough and allow to rise for 30 minutes. Place on floured baking board and knead thoroughly. Form into 10 buns, place on buttered baking sheet and allow to rise for 20 minutes. Bake in heated oven (Regulo 7—450° F.) for 6—10 minutes. When cool, slice off tops. Beat cream until stiff and mix in sugar and ground almonds. Divide between buns, place filling on cut part. Place back lid, sprinkle with icing sugar and serve in deep plates with hot milk.

SIBLING CAKE

Swedish

1 lb. flour	*Filling:*	2 oz. butter
½ pint milk		5 tablespoons sugar
1 oz. yeast		20 almonds
1 teaspoon sugar		5 tablespoons raisins
3 oz. butter		15 cardamoms
5 tablespoons sugar	*Garnish:*	10 chopped almonds,
		2 tablespoons coarse sugar
		beaten egg

Warm milk. Mix yeast with 1 teaspoon sugar. Mix flour, yeast and milk to smooth dough and allow to rise for 30 minutes. Beat butter and sugar until light and creamy and mix into dough. Knead dough until smooth, place on floured baking board and roll out into rectangles, ¼ inch thick. Melt 2 oz. butter and spread over dough. Scald, peel and chop almonds finely. Sprinkle over dough together with crushed cardamoms, sugar and raisins. Roll up and cut across into 2-inch pieces. Butter a round pan and sprinkle with flour. Place rolls close together, cut side up, and allow to rise for 20 minutes. Brush with beaten egg and sprinkle with chopped almonds and sugar. Bake in heated oven (Regulo 6—425 °F.) until golden.

SWEDISH PASTRIES

8 oz. butter	¼ teaspoon salt
½ pint milk	1 lb. flour
1 egg	1 beaten egg for garnish
2 tablespoons sugar	10 chopped almonds for garnish
1 oz. yeast	

Soften yeast in little milk. Beat eggs, salt and sugar. Work in flour, milk and yeast and knead dough until smooth. Place on floured baking board and roll out to ½ inch thick. Place butter in little lumps on dough and fold in 3 parts. Flatten by patting gently with roller. Fold dough again and roll out. Keep folding and rolling out until butter is well worked into dough. Roll out until one-third inch thick, cut into narrow strips and form into figure of eight or other interesting shapes. Place on buttered baking tray and allow to rise for 30 minutes. Brush with beaten egg and sprinkle with chopped almonds. Bake in heated oven (Regulo 8—475° F.) until golden.

SIMPLE PASTRIES

Swedish

3 tablespoons sugar	13 oz. self-raising flour
5 oz. butter	beaten egg for garnish
1 egg	sugar for garnish
7—10 tablespoons milk	icing sugar and water glaze

vanilla cream filling (see page 251).

Beat butter and sugar until light and fluffy. Stir in egg. Add milk and flour alternately, a little at a time, until all is worked in. Knead dough until smooth. Place on floured baking board and roll out until barely ¼ inch thick. Cut into 4 inch wide strips and place vanilla cream in line along centre. Fold 3 times lengthwise and cut into 3—4 inch pieces. Place on buttered baking sheet, folded side down. Brush with beaten egg and sprinkle with sugar. Bake in heated oven (Regulo 8—475° F.) until golden. Glaze with icing sugar and water and serve immediately.

DANISH PASTRY DOUGH

33—35 PASTRIES

1 lb. plain flour	½ pint milk
1 teaspoon salt	1 egg
4 tablespoons sugar	12 oz. butter
2¼ oz. yeast	

Sift flour and mix with sugar and salt. Mix yeast with a little cold milk and stir into flour, together with beaten egg, sugar and rest of milk. Stir wooden spoon until well mixed. Sprinkle a little flour on baking board and roll out dough until about ¾ inch thick. Stir butter until it has softened sufficiently to spread. Put a little on dough and spread over two-thirds of surface. Fold in plain part, then butter part, so that it is in 3 layers. Roll out again and repeat until all butter is folded in. Leave in cold place for 30 minutes.

SPANDAUER PASTRY

Danish

basic dough (see page 249) apple sauce (see page 219)
butter   *or* vanilla cream (see page 251)
sugar   *or* almond paste filling
egg white   (see page 251)

Roll out dough to ¼ inch thick. Mix equal portions of sugar and butter and spread over dough. Cut into 4 inch by 4 inch squares. Place 1 tablespoon filling in centre. Fold in all 4 corners so that they meet in middle and press down. Place on buttered baking sheet and leave in cold place for 20 minutes. Brush with egg white and bake in heated oven (Regulo 7—450° F.) until golden. Glaze with icing sugar and water.

COCK'S COMB PASTRY

Danish

basic dough (see page 249)   egg white
butter   chopped almonds
sugar   almond paste (see page 251)

Roll out dough until ¼ inch thick. Mix equal portions of sugar and butter and spread over dough. Cut dough into 4 inch by 4 inch squares. Place about 1 tablespoon almond paste across middle and fold over. Press edges together and make 4 cuts in outer edge. Place on buttered baking sheet and leave in cold place for 20 minutes. Brush with egg white, sprinkle with chopped almonds and sugar. Bake in heated oven (Regulo 7—450° F.) until golden.

CAKE FILLINGS

MOCCA CREAM

Swedish

2½ oz. unsalted butter   1 teaspoon vanilla essence
2 oz. icing sugar   2 tablespoons strong coffee
1 tablespoon cocoa

Stir butter until soft. Add sugar and cocoa, stirring until
well mixed. Add vanilla essence and coffee, drop by drop,
stirring vigorously until completely blended.

ALMOND PASTE

Danish

4 oz. butter   4 oz. ground almonds
4 oz. sugar

Mix all ingredients until well blended.

VANILLA CREAM

Swedish

1 egg   ½ pint milk
2 teaspoons potato flour   vanilla essence
1 tablespoon sugar

Put egg, flour and sugar in a saucepan and beat together.
Add milk while beating. Place on a medium flame and keep
beating until it simmers and is a smooth cream. Add vanilla
essence to taste. Let it cool and use as a filling for chocolate
cake.

BUTTER CREAM

Swedish

6 tablespoons sugar	4 tablespoons water
2 egg yolks	5 oz. butter

Put the sugar and water in a saucepan and simmer until sugar is melted. Pour over egg yolks and beat until cold. Then add butter a little at a time, stirring until it is all used and mixture is a smooth creamy consistency. This can be used as filling for chocolate cake or, better still, to spread over the top instead of icing.

CHOCOLATE CREAM

Swedish

6 tablespoons sugar	5 oz. butter
6 tablespoons water	3 tablespoons cocoa
2 egg yolks	

Put the sugar, cocoa and water in a saucepan and stir while it comes to the boil. Simmer while stirring until sugar is melted. Pour over egg yolks and stir until cool. Stir in butter, a little at a time, until it is all used and has a smooth creamy consistency. This can be used as a filling for cakes or to be spread on top in place of icing.

Scandinavians are known to enjoy a strong drink, aquavit and beer being the most popular. Hot punches and mulled wine are also popular and are particularly appreciated in the evening after skiing. These drinks seem to be specially associated with festivities and are eminently suitable for a Christmas or New Year's Eve party.

The tasty cool drinks need no special recommendation as they are always welcome anywhere.

CHAMPAGNE PUNCH

Swedish

10—12 SERVINGS

1 bottle champagne	3 tablespoons cognac
1 bottle hock	juice of 1 orange
1 bottle soda	cocktail cherries

Place cocktail cherries in ice tray, one in each compartment, fill with water and freeze. Chill all liquids. Mix in punch bowl and add orange juice. Place ice cubes in tall glasses with straws and serve punch.

HOT PUNCH OF AQUAVIT

Swedish

8—12 SERVINGS

1 bottle unspiced aquavit	4 cloves
3 oz. raisins	2 cinnamon sticks
3 oz. almonds	1 orange peel, candied
7 cardamoms	8 oz. lump sugar

Wash and dry raisins. Scald and peel almonds. Peel cardamoms. Take a decorative pot that can be used for serving, place all spices, raisins, almonds and orange peel in it and pour on aquavit. Cover and allow to stand for up to 1 hour. Heat punch just enough to enable it to light. Place sugar in wire basket over lighted punch and baste it with punch until sugar is melted. Place cover over it to put out flame. Serve immediately.

As this is a very potent drink, the number of guests it will serve depends on their stamina!

ICED RED WINE PUNCH

Swedish

6—8 SERVINGS

1 bottle red wine	1 lemon
3 tablespoons sherry	4 oz. grapes
3 tablespoons cognac	sugar to taste
1 bottle soda	ice
1 orange	

Chill liquids. Slice orange and lemon, discarding seeds and end pieces. Wash grapes, halve and de-seed them. Place some ice cubes in punch bowl. Pour in liquids. Stir in sugar to taste. Add fruit, serve in tall glasses with straws.

SIMPLE RED WINE PUNCH

Swedish

6 SERVINGS

1 bottle ordinary red wine	3 oz. sugar
1 bottle tonic or soda	pinch nutmeg
3 oz. cucumber	ice

Wash cucumber and slice very thinly. Place cucumber and sugar in layers in punch bowl. Pour on wine and let it stand in a cool place for about 1 hour. When ready to serve, add ice cubes, nutmeg and tonic or soda. Serve in tall glasses with straws.

SIMPLE WHITE WINE PUNCH

Swedish

6 SERVINGS

1 pint white wine	6 tablespoons sugar
1 pint water	4 oz. grapes
½ teaspoon nutmeg	ice

Wash and halve grapes, remove seeds. Place all ingredients in glass jug and chill for ½ hour. Add some ice cubes and serve. Excellent with a summer meal.

CHILLED SAUTERNE PUNCH

Swedish

6—8 SERVINGS

1 bottle Sauterne	1 lemon
4 tablespoons gin	cocktail cherries
½ pint soda	ice
1 orange	

Chill liquids. Just before serving pour into punch bowl and add ice. Slice orange and lemon, discarding seeds and ends, and add to punch. Add cherries and serve.

HOT RED WINE PUNCH

Swedish

4 SERVINGS

1 bottle ordinary red wine
3 tablespoons sherry
1 lemon

sugar to taste
½ teaspoon nutmeg

Wash and dry lemon. Cut off outer layer of peel. Pour wine and sherry into saucepan and add lemon peel, nutmeg and sugar to taste. Heat punch thoroughly, but do not let it boil. Serve very hot in thick glasses or mugs, with a lemon slice in each.

MULLED WINE

Swedish

8—12 SERVINGS

½ bottle unspiced aquavit
3 oz. raisins
½ bottle Bordeaux wine
3 oz. almonds
7 cardamoms

4 cloves
2 cinnamon sticks
1 orange peel, candied
6 oz. sugar

Wash and dry raisins. Scald and peel almonds. Peel cardamoms. Take a decorative pot that can be used for serving and place all the ingredients in it. Cover and let it stand for up to 1 hour. Heat, but do not let it boil. Stir to make sure sugar is melted. Serve in punch glasses.

HOT SAUTERNE PUNCH

Swedish

4—6 SERVINGS

1 bottle Sauterne	2 cloves
¼ pint cognac	4 oz. cube sugar
1 lemon	

Wash and dry lemon. Cut off outer layer of peel. Pour wine into saucepan and add sugar, cloves and lemon peel. Heat until a white foam is formed on top. Remove lemon peel. Heat cognac separately. Warm a punch bowl and mix hot wine and cognac in it. Slice lemon and place one piece in each glass or mug. Light punch and serve.

BEER BREAD

Norwegian

4 SERVINGS

1 pint light beer	½ pint cream
½ pint water	sugar to taste
2 egg yolks	croûtons or diced fried bread

Pour liquids into saucepan and add yolks. Heat slowly while whipping. Add sugar to taste. Remove from flame just before it comes to the boil. Serve immediately with croûtons or diced fried bread.

EGG TODDY

Swedish

1 SERVING

1 egg yolk   3 tablespoons cognac or sherry
2 tablespoons sugar   boiling water

This drink is served by placing egg yolk and sugar in a glass
with a spoon, so that each guest can prepare his own.

Egg and sugar are stirred until very white and porous.
Cognac is then added gradually while continuing to stir. The
glass is then topped with boiling water, stirred again and
is ready for drinking.

PINEAPPLE COBBLE

Swedish

6 SERVINGS

10 oz. tin pineapple cubes   cucumber peel
1 pint grapefruit juice   cocktail cherries
1 pint soda   sugar to taste
juice of ½ lemon   ice

Mix juices in glass jug and chill. Add pineapple cubes,
cucumber peel and ice, adding sugar to taste. Pour in soda.
Place 1 cherry in each glass and serve with straws.

ICED FRUIT TEA

Swedish

4—6 SERVINGS

5 oz. sugar
¾ pint water
½ pint cold, strong tea
juice of 3 lemons
juice of 3 oranges

10 oz. tin pineapple cubes
1 sliced orange
fresh berries
ice

Boil sugar and water until sugar is completely dissolved. When cold, mix in tea and fruit juices, pineapple and ice. Add orange slices and any fresh berries available. Serve in tall glasses with straws.

PARTY COFFEE

Swedish

4 SERVINGS

2 cups strong coffee
3 teaspoons cocoa
4 teaspoons sugar

4 teaspoons single cream
2 cups boiling water
whipped cream

Stir cocoa and sugar until mixed. Add single cream and stir until smooth. Add boiling water. Add heated coffee and serve with whipped cream.

INDEX OF RECIPES

INDEX

Mushroom sauce, 76
Mushroom sauce for fish dishes, 70
Mushroom soufflé, 117
Mushrooms, creamed, 102
Mushrooms, stewed, 102
Mustard mackerel, 132

Nut squares, 241
Nut sticks, 241

Oat cake with apples, 238
Oat leaves, 243
Omelette, 98
Onion casserole, 91
Onion sauce, 79, 80
Orange halves, filled, 215
Orange sauce, 85
Orange whip, 229

Pancake, apple, 224
Pancake, layer, 224
Pancakes, crisp, 223
Pancakes, filled, 99
Pancakes, Swedish, 221
Paprika sauce, 81
Parsnips, fried, 107
Parsnips, stewed, 106
Parson's ginger cake, 235
Party coffee, 260
Party herring, 134
Pastry, cock's comb, 250
Pastry dough, Danish, 249
Pastry, Spandauer, 250
Pea soup, 65, 66
Pea soup with bacon, 57
Pickled salt herring, 18
Pig's heart, stewed, 202
Pike, boiled, 164
Pineapple chiffon pudding, 226
Pineapple cobble, 259
Plum salad, 214
Plum surprise, 230
Poached cod, 154
Poor knights, 222
Pork and cabbage, 194
Pork chops, savoury, 192
Pork, fried, 196
Pork, potroast, 193
Pork, roast, with prunes, 192
Pork, rolled, with red cabbage, 195
Pork, stuffed rolls, 194

Potato cakes, 104
Potato salad, 45
Potato and tomato salad, 44
Potatoes, fried, 103, 104
Potatoes, roast, with cheese, 105
Potatoes stuffed with herring, 143
Potroast of pork, 193
Potroast, Swedish, 180
Potroasted veal, 203
Poultry sandwich, 54
Punch of aquavit, 254
Purée of carrots, 107
Purée of swede, 109

Quick cake, 234

Rabbit in cream sauce, 212
Raisin cuts, 244
Raspberry cream, 218
Raw beef, 28
Raw vegetable salad, 37
Red cabbage, 113
Red cole slaw, 41
Red porridge, 218
Red wine punch, iced, 255
Red wine sauce, 77
Rhubard cream, 217
Rice porridge, 222
Roast goose, 208
Roast leg of lamb, 187
Roast pork with prunes, 192
Roast potatoes with cheese, 105
Roast venison, 211
Roasted spareribs, 196
Rolled beef with anchovy stuffing, 178
Rolled fish fillets, 165
Rolled pork with red cabbage, 195
Rolled veal with mushroom stuffing, 186

Sailor's beef, 184
Sailor ring, 243
Salmon, boiled, 167
Salmon butter and asparagus sandwich, 51
Salmon, marinated, 23
Salt beef sandwich, 54
Sandwich with boiled fish and mayonnaise, 48
Sandwich with cheese butter, 48

Tomato and mushroom sauce, 75
Tomatoes stuffed with mushrooms, 93
Tomato sauce, 76
Tomato soup, 56, 57
Tuesday soup, 62

Vanilla biscuits, 242
Vanilla cream, 251
Vanilla sauce, 82
Veal birds, 186
Veal, boiled, with dill sauce, 188
Veal chops with mushrooms, 204
Veal cutlet, minced, 212
Veal cutlet Oscar, 185
Veal fillet, stuffed, 204
Veal fricassee, 189
Veal and pork meatballs for soup, 61
Veal, potroasted, 203
Veal, rolled, with mushroom stuffing, 186

Vegetable salad, 37, 38
Vegetable soufflé, 118
Vegetable soup, 60, 61
Vegetables au gratin, 116
Venison, roast, 211

Waffles, 223
West Coast herring casserole, 136
White cabbage, stewed, 113
White cole slaw, 43
White wine punch, 256
Whiting, baked, with cheese sauce, 174
Whiting baked with mustard, 146
Whiting baked with tomatoes, 146
Whiting baked with vegetables, 145
Whiting, stewed, 147
Whole fried onions, 110
Wine sauce, 85
Winter pea soup, 65